C000172010

Python:

3 books in 1

Beginner's guide, Data science and Machine learning.

The easiest guide to get started in Python programming.
Unlock your programmer potential and develop your
project in just 30 days.

William Dimick

PYTHON FOR BEGINNERS:

The survival guide to start programming from scratch. Get involved in the learning process, master Python code and reach your goals now without efforts.

William Dimick

Introduction

So, you have heard about a language that everyone considers amazing, easy and fast... the language of the future. You sit with your friends, and all they have to talk about is essentially gibberish to you, and yet it seems interesting to the rest of them. Perhaps you plan to lead a business, and a little research into things reveals that a specific language is quite a lot in demand these days. Sure enough, you can hire someone to do the job for you, but how would you know if the job is being done the way you want it to be, top-notch in quality and original in nature?

Whether you aim to pursue a career out of this journey, you are about to embark on or set up your own business to serve hundreds of thousands of clients who are looking for someone like you; you need to learn Python.

When it comes to Python, there are so many videos and tutorials which you can find online. The problem is that each seems to be heading in a different direction. There is no way to tell which structure you need to follow, or where you should begin and where should it end. There is a good possibility you might come across a video that seemingly answers your call, only to find out that the narrator is not explaining much and pretty much all you see, you have to guess what it does.

I have seen quite a few tutorials like that myself. They can be annoying and some even misleading. Some programmers will tell you that you are already too late to learn Python and that you will not garner the kind of success you seek out for yourself. Let me put such rumors and ill-messages to rest.

- Age – It is just a number. What truly matters are the desire you have to learn. You do not need to be X years old to learn this effectively. Similarly, there is no upper limit of Y years for the learning process. You can be 60 and still be able to learn the language and execute brilliant commands. All it requires is a mind that is ready to learn and a piece of good knowledge on how to operate a computer, open and close programs, and download stuff from the internet. That's it!

- Language – Whether you are a native English speaker or a non-native one, the language is open for all. As long as you can form basic sentences and make sense out of them, you should easily be able to understand the language of Python itself. It follows something called the "clean-code" concept, which effectively promotes the readability of codes.

- Python is two decades old already – If you are worried that you are two decades late, let me remind you that Python is a progressive language in nature. That means, every year, we find new additions to the language of Python, and some obsolete components are removed as well. Therefore, the concept of "being too late" already stands void. You can learn today, and you will already be familiar with every command by the end of a year. Whatever has existed so far, you will already know. What would follow then, you will eventually pick up. There is no such thing as being too late to learn Python.

Of course, some people are successful and some not. Everything boils down to how effectively and creatively you use the language to execute problems and solutions. The more original your program is, the better you fare off.

"I vow that I will give my best to learn the language of Python and master the basics. I also promise to practice writing codes and programs after I am done with this book."

Bravo! You just took the first step. Now, we are ready to turn the clock back a little and see exactly where Python came from. If you went through the introduction, I gave you a brief on how Python came into existence, but I left out quite a few parts. Let us look into those and see why Python was the need of the hour.

Before the inception of Python, and the famous language that it has gone on to become, things were quite different. Imagine a world where programmers gathered from across the globe in a huge computer lab. You have some of the finest minds from the planet, working together towards a common goal, whatever that might be. Naturally, even the finest intellectuals can end up making mistakes.

Suppose one such programmer ended up creating a program, and he is not too sure of what went wrong. The room is full of other programmers, and sure enough, approaching someone for assistance would be the first thought of the day. The programmer approaches another busy person who gladly decides to help out a fellow intellectual programmer. Within that brief walk from one station to the other, the programmer quickly exchanges the information, which seems to be a common error. It is only when the programmer views the code that they are caught off-guard. This fellow member has no idea what any of the code does. The variables are labeled with what can only be defined as encryptions. The words do not make any sense, nor is there any way to find out where the error lies.

The compiler continues to throw in error after error. Remember, this was well before 1991 when people did not have IDEs, which would help them see where the error is and what needs to be done. The entire exercise would end up wasting hours upon hours just to figure out that a semi-colon was missing. Embarrassing and time-wasting!

This was just a small example, imagine the entire thing but on a global scale. The programming community struggled to find ways to write codes that could be understood easily by others. Some languages supported some syntaxes, while others did not. These languages would not necessarily work in harmony with each other, either. The world of programming was a mess. Had Python not come at the opportune moment that it did, things would have been so much more difficult for us to handle.

Guido Van Rossum, a Dutch-programmer, decided to work on a pet project. Yes, you read that, right! Mr. Van Rossum wanted to keep himself occupied during the holiday season and, hence, decided to write a new interpreter for a language he had been thinking of lately. He decided to call the language Python, and contrary to popular belief, it has nothing to do with the reptile itself. Tracing its root from its predecessor, the ABC, Python came into existence just when it was needed.

For our non-programming friends, ABC is the name of an old programming language. Funny as it may sound, naming conventions wasn't exactly the strongest here.

Python was quickly accepted by the programming community, albeit there is the fact that programmers were a lot less numerous back then. It's revolutionary user-friendliness, responsive nature and adaptability immediately caught the attention of everyone around. The more people vested their time into this new language, the more Mr. Van Rossum started investing his resources and knowledge to enhance the experience further. Within a short period, Python was competing against the then leading languages of the world. It soon went on to outlive quite a few of them owing to the core concept is brought to the table: ease of readability. Unlike any other programming language of that time, Python delivered codes that were phenomenally easy to read and understand right away.

Remember our friend, the programmer, who asked for assistance? If he were to do that now, the other fellow would immediately understand what was going on.

Python also acquired fame for being a language that had an object-oriented approach. This opened more usability of the language to the programmers who required an effective way to manipulate objects. Think of a simple game. Anything you see within it is an object that behaves in a certain way. Giving that object that 'sense' is object-oriented programming (OOP). Python was able to pull that off rather easily. Python is considered as a multi-paradigm language, with OOP being a part of that as well.

Fast forward to the world we live in, and Python continues to dominate some of the cutting-edge technologies in existence. With real-world applications and a goliath of a contribution to aspects like machine learning, data sciences, and analytics, Python is leading the charge with full force.

An entire community of programmers has dedicated their careers to maintain Python and develop it as time goes by. As for the founder, Mr. Van Rossum initially accepted the title of Benevolent Dictator for Life (BDFL) and retired on 12 July 2018. This title was bestowed upon Mr. Van Rossum by the Python community.

Today, Python 3 is the leading version of the language alongside Python 2, which has its days numbered. You do not need to learn both of these to succeed. We will begin with the latest version of Python as almost everything that was involved in the previous version was carried forward, except for components that were either dull or useless.

I know, right about now you are rather eager to dive into the concepts and get done with history. It is vital for us to learn a few things about the language and why it came into existence in the first place. This information might be useful at some point in time, especially if you were to look at various codes and identify which one of those was written in Python and which one was not.

For anyone who may have used languages like C, C++, C#, JavaScript, you might find quite a few similarities within Python, and some major improvements too. Unlike in most of these languages, where you need to use a semicolon to let the compiler know that the line has ended, Python needs none of that. Just press enter and the program immediately understands that the line has ended.

Before we do jump ahead, remember how some skeptics would have you believe it is too late to learn Python? It is because of Python that self-driving cars are coming into existence. Has the world seen too much of them already? When was the last time you saw one of these vehicles on the road? This is just one of a gazillion possibilities that lay ahead for us to conquer. All it needs is for us to learn the language, brush up our skills, and get started.

"A journey to a thousand miles begins with the first step. After that, you are already one step closer to your destination."

Chapter 1: Installing Python

Python can be obtained from the Python Software Foundation website at python.org. Typically, that involves downloading the appropriate installer for your operating system and running it on your machine. Some operating systems, notably Linux, provide a package manager that can be run to install Python.

Python is available on a wide variety of platforms including Linux and Mac OS X. Let's understand how to set up our Python environment.

Local Environment Setup

Open a terminal window and type "python" to find out if it is already installed and which version is installed.

- Unix (Solaris, Linux, FreeBSD, AIX, HP/UX, SunOS, IRIX, etc.)

- Win 9x/NT/2000

- Macintosh (Intel, PPC, 68K)

- OS/2

- DOS (multiple versions)

- PalmOS

- Nokia mobile phones

- Windows CE

- Acorn/RISC OS

- BeOS

- Amiga

- VMS/OpenVMS

- QNX

- VxWorks

- Psion

Python has also been ported to the Java and .NET virtual machines

Getting Python

The most up-to-date and current source code, binaries, documentation, news, etc., is available on the official website of Python https://www.python.org/

You can download Python documentation from https://www.python.org/doc/. The documentation is available in HTML, PDF, and PostScript formats.

Installing Python

Python distribution is available for a wide variety of platforms. You need to download only the binary code applicable for your platform and install Python. If the binary code for your platform is not available, you need a C compiler to compile the source code manually. Compiling the source code offers more flexibility in terms of choice of features that you require in your installation.

Here Is A Quick Overview Of Installing Python On Various Platforms:

Unix And Linux Installation

Here are the simple steps to install Python on Unix/Linux machine.

- Open a Web browser and go to https://www.python.org/downloads/.

- Follow the link to download zipped source code available for Unix/Linux.

- Download and extract files.

- Editing the Modules/Setup file if you want to customize some options.

- Run. /configure script

- Make install

- This installs Python at standard location /usr/local/bin and its libraries at /usr/local/lib/pythonxx where XX is the version of Python.

Windows Installation

Here are the steps to install Python on Windows machine.

- Open a Web browser and go to https://www.python.org/downloads/.

- Follow the link for the Windows installer python-XYZ.msi file where XYZ is the version you need to install.

- To use this installer python-XYZ.msi, the Windows system must support Microsoft Installer 2.0. Save the installer file to your local machine and then run it to find out if your machine supports MSI.

- Run the downloaded file. This brings up the Python install wizard, which is really easy to use. Just accept the default settings, wait until the install is finished, and you are done.

Macintosh Installation

Recent Macs come with Python installed, but it may be several years out of date. See http://www.python.org/download/mac/ for instructions on getting the current version along with extra tools to support development on the Mac. For older Mac OS's before Mac OS X 10.3 (released in 2003), MacPython is available.

Setting Up PATH

Programs and other executable files can be in many directories, so operating systems provide a search path that lists the directories that the OS searches for executables.

The path is stored in an environment variable, which is a named string maintained by the operating system. This variable contains information available to the command shell and other programs. The path variable is named as PATH in Unix or Path in Windows (Unix is case sensitive; Windows is not).

In Mac OS, the installer handles the path details. To invoke the Python interpreter from any particular directory, you must add the Python directory to your path.

Setting Path at Unix/Linux

To add the python directory to the path for a particular session in Unix:

- In the csh shell – type sentence PATH "$PATH:/usr/local/bin/python" and press Enter.

- In the bash shell (Linux) – type export PATH="$PATH:/usr/local/bin/python" and press Enter.

- In the sh or ksh shell – type PATH="$PATH:/usr/local/bin/python" and press Enter.

- Note – /usr/local/bin/python is the path of the Python directory

Setting Path At Windows

To add the Python directory to the path for a particular session in Windows:

- At the command prompt – type path %path%; C:\Python and press Enter.

- Note – C:\Python is the path of the Python directory

Python Environment Variables

Here are important environment variables, which can be recognized by Python:

Sr.No.	Variable	Description
1	PYTHONPATH	It has a role similar to PATH. This variable tells the Python interpreter

		where to locate the module files imported into a program. It should include the Python source library directory and the directories containing Python source code. PYTHONPATH is sometimes preset by the Python installer
2	PYTHONSTARTUP	It contains the path of an initialization file containing Python source code. It is executed every time you start the interpreter. It is named as. pythonrc.py in Unix and it contains commands that load utilities or modify PYTHONPATH.
3	PYTHONCASEOK	It is used in Windows to instruct Python to find the first case-insensitive match in an import statement. Set this

		variable to any value to activate it.
4	PYTHONHOME	It is an alternative module search path. It is usually embedded in the PYTHONSTARTUP or PYTHONPATH directories to make switching module libraries easy.

Running Python

There are three different ways to start Python:

Interactive Interpreter

You can start Python from Unix, DOS, or any other system that provides you a command-line interpreter or shell window.

Enter python the command line.

Start coding right away in the interactive interpreter.

- $python # Unix/Linux

    o or

- python% # Unix/Linux

- o   or

- C:> python # Windows/DOS

Here is the list of all the available command line options:

Sr.No.	Option	Description
1	-d	It provides debug output.
2	-O	It generates optimized bytecode (resulting in. pyo files).
3	-S	Do not run import site to look for Python paths on startup.
4	-v	Verbose output (detailed trace on import statements).

5	-X	Disable class-based built-in exceptions (just use strings); obsolete starting with version 1.6.
6	-c cmd	Run Python script sent in as cmd string
7	File	Run Python script from given file

Script from The Command-Line

A Python script can be executed at command line by invoking the interpreter on your application, as in the following:

- $python script.py # Unix/Linux

  o or

- python% script.py # Unix/Linux

  o or

- C: >python script.py # Windows/DOS

Note*:* Be sure the file permission mode allows execution.

Integrated Development Environment

You can run Python from a Graphical User Interface (GUI) environment as well, if you have a GUI application on your system that supports Python.

- Unix: IDLE is the very first Unix IDE for Python.

- Windows: PythonWin is the first Windows interface for Python and is an IDE with a GUI.

- Macintosh: The Macintosh version of Python along with the IDLE IDE is available from the main website, downloadable as either MacBinary or BinHex'd files.

If you are not able to set up the environment properly, then you can take help from your system admin. Make sure the Python environment is properly set up and working perfectly fine.

Note*:* All the examples given in subsequent chapters are executed with Python 2.4.3 version available on CentOS flavor of Linux.

IDLE

What Is Python IDLE?

Every Python installation comes with an Integrated Development and Learning Environment, which you'll see shortened to IDLE or even IDE. These are a class of applications that help you write code more efficiently. While there are many IDEs for you to choose from, Python IDLE is very bare-bones, which makes it the perfect tool for a beginning programmer.

Python IDLE comes included in Python installations on Windows and Mac. If you're a Linux user, then you should be able to find and download Python IDLE using your package manager. Once you've installed it, you can then use Python IDLE as an interactive interpreter or as a file editor.

IDLE is intended to be a simple IDE and suitable for beginners, especially in an educational environment. To that end, it is cross-platform, and avoids feature clutter. According to the included README, its main features are:

- Multi-window text editor with syntax highlighting, autocompletion, smart indent and other.

- Python shell with syntax highlighting.

- Integrated debugger with stepping, persistent breakpoints, and call stack visibility.

A File Editor
Every programmer needs to be able to edit and save text files. Python programs are files with the .py extension that

contain lines of Python code. Python IDLE gives you the ability to create and edit these files with ease.

Python IDLE also provides several useful features that you'll see in professional IDEs, like basic syntax highlighting, code completion, and auto-indentation. Professional IDEs are more robust pieces of software and they have a steep learning curve. If you're just beginning your Python programming journey, then Python IDLE is a great alternative!

Editing A File

Once you've opened a file in Python IDLE, you can then make changes to it. When you're ready to edit a file, you'll see something like this:

- An opened python file in IDLE containing a single line of code

- The contents of your file are displayed in the open window. The bar along the top of the window contains three pieces of important information:

- The name of the file that you're editing

- The full path to the folder where you can find this file on your computer

- The version of Python that IDLE is using

In the image above, you're editing the file myFile.py, which is located in the Documents folder. The Python version is 3.7.1, which you can see in parentheses.

There are also two numbers in the bottom right corner of the window:

- Ln: shows the line number that your cursor is on.

- Col: shows the column number that your cursor is on.

It's useful to see these numbers so that you can find errors more quickly. They also help you make sure that you're staying within a certain line width. There are a few visual cues in this window that will help you remember to save your work. If you look closely, then you'll see that Python IDLE uses asterisks to let you know that your file has unsaved changes:

- Shows what an unsaved file looks like in the idle editor

The file name shown in the top of the IDLE window is surrounded by asterisks. This means that there are unsaved changes in your editor. You can save these changes with your system's standard keyboard shortcut, or you can select File → Save from the menu bar. Make sure that you save your file with the. py extension so that syntax highlighting will be enabled.

How to Improve Your Workflow

Now that you've seen how to write, edit, and execute files in Python IDLE, it's time to speed up your workflow! The Python IDLE editor offers a few features that you'll see in most professional IDEs to help you code faster. These features include automatic indentation, code completion and call tips, and code context.

Chapter 2: Python Loops and Numbers

Loops

In general, statements are executed sequentially: The first statement in a function is executed first, followed by the second, and so on. There may be a situation when you need to execute a block of code several number of times.

Programming languages provide various control structures that allow for more complicated execution paths. A loop statement allows us to execute a statement or group of statements multiple times. The following diagram illustrates a loop statement.

Loop Architecture

Python programming language provides following types of loops to handle looping requirements.

SR No.	Loop Type	Description
1	1 while loop	Repeats a statement or group of statements while a given condition is TRUE. It tests the condition before executing the loop body.

2	for loop	Executes a sequence of statements multiple times and abbreviates the code that manages the loop variable.
3	Nested loops	You can use one or more loop inside any another while, for or do. while loop.

Loop Control Statements

Loop control statements change execution from its normal sequence. When execution leaves a scope, all automatic objects that were created in that scope are destroyed. Python supports the following control statements. Click the following links to check their detail.

Let us go through the loop control statements briefly.

SR No.	Control Statement	Description
1	break statement	Terminates the loop statement and transfers execution to the statement immediately following the loop.
2	continue statement	Causes the loop to skip the remainder of its body and immediately retest its condition prior to reiterating.
3	pass statement	The pass statement in Python is used when a statement is required syntactically but you do not want any command or code to execute.

Numbers

Number data types store numeric values. They are immutable data types, means that changing the value of a number data type results in a newly allocated object. Number objects are created when you assign a value to them. For example:

- var1 = 1

- var2 = 10

You can also delete the reference to a number object by using the del statement. The syntax of the del statement is:

Del var1[, var2[, var3[...., varN]

You can delete a single object or multiple objects by using the del statement. For example:

- Del var

- Del var_a, var_b

Python Supports Four Different Numerical Types

1. Int (Signed Integers): They are often called just integers or ints, are positive or negative whole numbers with no decimal point.

2. Long (Long Integers): Also called longs, they are integers of unlimited size, written like integers and followed by an uppercase or lowercase L.

3. Float (Floating Point Real Values): Also called floats, they represent real numbers and are written with a decimal point dividing the integer and fractional parts. Floats may also be in scientific notation, with E or e indicating the power of 10 (2.5e2 = 2.5 x 102 = 250).

4. Complex (Complex Numbers): are of the form a + bJ, where a and b are floats and J (or j) represents the square root of -1 (which is an imaginary number). The real part of the number is a, and the imaginary part is b. Complex numbers are not used much in Python programming.

Examples

Here Are Some Examples Of Numbers

- int long float complex

- 10 51924361L 0.0 3.14j

- 100 -0x19323L 15.20 45. j

- -786 0122L -21.9 9.322e-36j

- 080 0xDEFABCECBDAECBFBAEL 32.3+e18 .876j

- -0490 535633629843L -90. -.6545+0J

- -0x260 -052318172735L -32.54e100 3e+26J

- 0x69 -4721885298529L 70.2-E12 4.53e-7j

Python allows you to use a lowercase L with long, but it is recommended that you use only an uppercase L to avoid confusion with the number 1. Python displays long integers with an uppercase L.

A complex number consists of ordered pair of real floating point numbers denoted by a + bj, where a is the real part and b is the imaginary part of the complex number.

Number Type Conversion

Python converts numbers internally in an expression containing mixed types to a common type for evaluation. But sometimes, you need to coerce a number explicitly from one type to another to satisfy the requirements of an operator or function parameter.

- Type int(x) to convert x to a plain integer.

- Type long(x) to convert x to a long integer.

- Type float(x) to convert x to a floating-point number.

- Type complex(x) to convert x to a complex number with real part x and imaginary part zero.

- Type complex (x, y) to convert x and y to a complex number with real part x and imaginary part y. x and y are numeric expressions

Mathematical Functions →

Python includes following functions that perform mathematical calculations.

SR.NO	Functions and Return	Description
1	abs(x)	The absolute value of x: the (positive) distance between x and zero.
2	ceil(x)	The ceiling of x: the smallest integer not less than x
3	cmp (x, y)	-1 if x < y, 0 if x == y, or 1 if x > y
4	exp(x)	The exponential of x: ex

5	modf(x)	The fractional and integer parts of x in a two-item tuple. Both parts have the same sign as x. The integer part is returned as a float.
6	floor(x)	The floor of x: the largest integer not greater than x
7	log(x)	The natural logarithm of x, for x> 0
8	log10(x)	The base-10 logarithm of x for x> 0.
9	max (x1, x2,)	The largest of its arguments: the value closest to positive infinity.

10	min (x1, x2,)	The smallest of its arguments: the value closest to negative infinity.
11	modf(x)	The fractional and integer parts of x in a two-item tuple. Both parts have the same sign as x. The integer part is returned as a float.
12	pow (x, y)	The value of x**y.
13	round (x [, n])	x rounded to n digits from the decimal point. Python rounds away from zero as a tie-breaker: round (0.5)

		is 1.0 and round (-0.5) is -1.0.
14	14 sqrt(x)	The square root of x for x > 0

Random Number Functions

Random numbers are used for games, simulations, testing, security, and privacy applications. Python includes following functions that are commonly used.

SR.NO.	Functions	Description
1	choice(seq)	A random item from a list, tuple, or string.
2	randrange	([start,] stop [, step]) A randomly selected element from range (start, stop, step)

3	random ()	A random float r, such that 0 is less than or equal to r and r is less than 1
4	seed([x])	Sets the integer starting value used in generating random numbers. Call this function before calling any other random module function. Returns None.
5	shuffle(lst)	Randomizes the items of a list in place. Returns None.
6	uniform (x, y)	A random float r, such that x is less than or equal to r and r is less than y

Trigonometric Functions

Python includes following functions that perform trigonometric calculations.

SR.NO	Functions	Description
1	acos(x)	Return the arc cosine of x, in radians.
2	asin(x)	Return the arc sine of x, in radians.
3	atan(x)	Return the arc tangent of x, in radians.
4	atan2(y, x)	Return atan (y / x), in radians.
5	cos(x)	Return the cosine of x radians.

6	hypot (x, y)	Return the Euclidean norm, sqrt (x*x + y*y).
7	sin(x)	Return the sine of x radians.
8	tan(x)	Return the tangent of x radians.
9	degrees(x)	Converts angle x from radians to degrees.

Mathematical Constants

The module also defines two mathematical constants:

SR.No.	Constants	Description
1	pi	The mathematical constant pi.

2	e	The mathematical constant e

Chapter 3: Data Types

Computer programming languages have several different methods of storing and interacting with data, and these different methods of representation are the data types you'll interact with. The primary data types within Python are integers, floats, and strings. These data types are stored in Python using different data structures: lists, tuples, and dictionaries. We'll get into data structures after we broach the topic of data types.

Integers in Python is not different from what you were taught in math class: a whole number or a number that possess no decimal points or fractions. Numbers like 4, 9, 39, -5, and 1215 are all integers. Integers can be stored in variables just by using the assignment operator, as we have seen before.

Floats are numbers that possess decimal parts. This makes numbers like -2.049, 12.78, 15.1, and 1.01 floats. The method of creating a float instance in Python is the same as declaring an integer: just choose a name for the variable and then use the assignment operator.

While we've mainly dealt with numbers so far, Python can also interpret and manipulate text data. Text data is referred to as a "string," and you can think of it as the letters that are strung together in a word or series of words. To create an instance of a string in Python, you can use either double quotes or single quotes.

string_1 = "This is a string."

string_2 = 'This is also a string.'

However, while either double or single quotes can be used, it is recommended that you use double quotes when possible. This is because there may be times you need to nest quotes within quotes, and using the traditional format of single quotes within double quotes is the encouraged standard.

Something to keep in mind when using strings is that numerical characters surrounded by quotes are treated as a string and not as a number.

The 97 here is a string

Stringy = "97"

Here it is a number

Numerical = 97

String Manipulation

When it comes to manipulating strings, we can combine strings in more or less the exact way we combine numbers.

All you must do is insert an additional operator in between two strings to combine them. Try replicating the code below:

Str_1 = "Words "

Str_2 = "and "

Str_3 = "more words."

Str_4 = Str_1 + Str_2 + Str_3

print (Str_4)

What you should get back is: "Words and more words."

Python provides many easy-to-use, built-in commands you can use to alter strings. For instance, adding. upper () to a string will make all characters in the string uppercase while using. lower () on the string will make all the characters in the string lowercase. These commands are called "functions," and we'll go into them in greater detail, but for now know that Python has already done much of the heavy lifting for you when it comes to manipulating strings.

String Formatting

Other methods of manipulating strings include string formatting accomplished with the "%" operator. The fact that the "%" symbol returns remainders when carrying out mathematical operations, but it has another use when working with strings. In the context of strings, however, the % symbol allows you to specify values/variables you would like to insert into a string and then have the string filled in with those values in specified areas. You can think of it like sorting a bunch of labeled items (the values beyond the % symbol) into bins (the holes in the string you've marked with %).

Try running this bit of code to see what happens:

```
String_to_print = "With the modulus operator, you can add %s, integers like %d, or even floats like %2.1f." % ("strings", 25, 12.34)

print (String_to_print)
```

The output of the print statement should be as follows:

"With the modulus operator, you can add strings, integers like 25, or even float like 12.3."

The "s" modifier after the % is used to denote the placement of strings, while the "d" modifier is used to indicate the placement of integers. Finally, the "f" modifier is used to indicate the placement of floats, and the decimal notation between the "%" and "f" is used to declare how many columns need to be displayed. For instance, if the modulator is used like this %2.1, it means you need two columns after the decimal place and one column before the decimal place displayed.

There's another way to format strings in Python. You can use the built-in "format" function. We'll go into what functions are exactly. Still, Python provides us with a handy shortcut to avoid having to type out the modulus operator whenever we want to format a string. Instead, we can just write something like the following:

"The string you want to format {}". format (values you want to insert).

The braces denote wherein the string you want to insert the value, and to insert multiple values, all you need to do is create multiple braces and then separate the values with commas. In other words, you would type something like this:

String_to_print = "With the modulus operator, you can add {0: s}, integers like {1: d}, or even floats like {2:2.2f}."

print (String_to_print. format ("strings", 25, 12.34))

Inside the brackets goes the data type tag and the position of the value in the collection of values you want to place in that spot. Try shifting the numbers in the brackets above around and see how they change. Remember that Python, unlike some other programming languages, is a zero-based system when it comes to positions, meaning that the first item in a list of items is always said to be at position zero/0 and not one/1.

One last thing to mention about string formatting in Python is that if you are using the format function and don't care to indicate where a value should go manually, you can simply leave the brackets blank. Doing so will have Python automatically fill in the brackets, in order from left to right, with the values in your list ordered from left to right (the first bracket gets the first item in the list, the second bracket gets the second item, etc.).

Type Casting

The term "type casting" refers to the act of converting data from one type to another type. As you program, you may often find out that you need to convert data between types. There are three helpful commands that Python has which allow the quick and easy conversion between data types: int (), float () and str ().

All three of the above commands convert what is placed within the parenthesis to the data type outside the parentheses. This means that to convert a float into an integer, you would write the following:

int (float here)

Because integers are whole numbers, anything after the decimal point in a float is dropped when it is converted into an integer. (Ex. 3.9324 becomes 3, 4.12 becomes 4.) Note that you cannot convert a non-numerical string into an integer, so typing: int ("convert this") would throw an error.

The float () command can convert integers or certain strings into floats. Providing either an integer or an integer in quotes (a string representation of an integer) will convert the provided value into a float. Both 5 and "5" become 5.0.

Finally, the str () function is responsible for the conversion of integers and floats to strings. Plug any numerical value into the parenthesis and get back a string representation of it.

We've covered a fair amount of material so far. Before we go any farther, let's do an exercise to make sure that we understand the material we've covered thus far.

Assignment and Formatting Exercise

Here's an assignment. Write a program that does the following:

- Assigns a numerical value to a variable and changes the value in some way.

- Assigns a string value to some variable.

- Prints the string and then the value using string formatting.

- Converts the numerical data into a different format and prints the new data form.

Give it your best shot before looking below for an example of how this could be done.

Ready to see an example of how that could be accomplished?

R = 9

R = 9 / 3

stringy = "There will be a number following this sentence: {}". format(R)

print(stringy)

R = str(R)

print(R)

Chapter 4: Variable in Python

When writing complex codes, your program will demand data essential to conduct changes when you proceed with your executions. Variables are, therefore, sections used to store code values created after you assign a value during program development. Python, unlike other related language programming software, lacks the command to declare a variable as they change after being set. Besides, Python values are undefined like in most cases of programming in other computer languages.

Variation in Python is therefore described as memory reserves used for storing data values. As such, Python variables act as storage units, which feed the computer with the necessary data for processing. Each value comprises of its database in Python programming, and every data are categorized as Numbers, Tuple, Dictionary, and List, among others. As a programmer, you understand how variables work and how helpful they are in creating an effective program using Python. As such, the tutorial will enable learners to understand declare, re-declare, and concatenate, local and global variables as well as how to delete a variable.

Variable Vs. Constants

Variables and constants are two components used in Python programming but perform separate functions. Variables, as well as constants, utilize values used to create codes to execute during program creation. Variables act as essential storage locations for data in the memory, while constants are variables whose value remains unchanged. In comparison, variables store reserves for data while constants are a type of variable files with consistent values written in capital letters and separated by underscores.

Variables Vs. Literals

Variables also are part of literals which are raw data fed on either variable or constant with several literals used in Python programming. Some of the common types of literals used include Numeric, String, and Boolean, Special and Literal collections such as Tuple, Dict, List, and Set. The difference between variables and literals arises where both deal with unprocessed data but variables store the while laterals feed the data to both constants and variables.

Variables Vs. Arrays

Python variables have a unique feature where they only name the values and store them in the memory for quick retrieval and supplying the values when needed. On the other hand, Python arrays or collections are data types used in programming language and categorized into a list, tuple, set, and dictionary. When compared to variables, the array tends to provide a platform to include collectives functions when written while variables store all kinds of data intended. When choosing your charming collection, ensure you select the one that fits your requirements henceforth meaning retention of meaning, enhancing data security and efficiency.

Classifications of Python Arrays Essential for Variables

Lists

Python lists offer changeable and ordered data and written while accompanying square brackets, for example, "an apple," "cherry." Accessing an already existing list by referring to the index number while with the ability to write negative indexes such as '-1' or '-2'. You can also maneuver within your list and select a specific category of indexes by first determining your starting and endpoints. The return value with therefore be the range of specified items. You can also specify a scale of negative indexes, alter the value of the current item, loop between items on the list, add or remove items, and confirming if items are available.

Naming Variables

The naming of variables remains straightforward, and both beginners and experienced programmers can readily perform the process. However, providing titles to these variables accompany specific rules to ensure the provision of the right name. Consistency, style, and adhering to variable naming rules ensure that you create an excellent and reliable name to use both today and the future. The rules are:

- Names must have a single word, that is, with no spaces

- Names must only comprise of letters and numbers as well as underscores such as (_)

- The first letter must never be a number

- Reserved words must never be used as variable names

When naming variables, you should bear in mind that the system is case-sensitive, hence avoid creating the same names within a single program to prevent confusion. Another important component when naming is considering the style. It entails beginning the title with a lowercase letter while using underscores as spaces between your words or phrases used. Besides, the program customarily prevents starting the name with a capital letter. Begin with a lowercase letter and either mix or use them consistently.

When creating variable names, it may seem so straightforward and easy, but sometimes it may become verbose henceforth becoming a disaster to beginners. However, the challenge of creating sophisticated names is quite beneficial for learned as it prepares you for the following tutorials. Similarly, Python enables you to write your desired name of any length consisting of lower- and upper-case letters, numbers as well as underscores. Python also offers the addition of complete Unicode support essential for Unicode features in variables.

Specific rules are governing the procedure for naming variables; hence adhere to them to create an exceptional name to your variables. Create more readable names that have meaning to prevent instances of confusion to your members, especially programmers. A more descriptive name is much preferred compares to others. However, the technique of naming variables remains illegible as different programmers decide on how they are going to create their kind of names.

Learning Python Strings, Numbers and Tuple

Python strings are part of Python variables and comprise of objects created from enclosing characters or values in double-quotes. For example, 'var = Hello World'. With Python not supporting character types in its functions, they are however treated as strings of one more character as well as substrings. Within the Python program, there exist several string operators making it essential for variables to be named and stored in different formats. Some of the string operators commonly used in Python are [], [:], 'in', r/R, %, +, and *.

There exist several methods of strings today. Some include replacing Python string () to return a copy of the previous value in a variable, changing the string format, that is, upper and lower cases, and using the 'join' function, especially for concatenating variables. Other methods include the reverse function and split strings using the command' word. split'. What to note is that strings play an important role, especially in naming and storage of values despite Python strings being immutable.

On the other hand, Python numbers are categorized into three main types; that is, int, float, and complex. Variable numbers are usually created when assigning a value for them. For instance, int values are generally whole numbers with unlimited length and are either positive or negative such as 1, 2, and 3. Float numbers also either positive or negative and may have one or more decimals like 2.1, 4.3, and 1.1 while complex numbers comprise both of a letter 'j' as the imaginary portion and numbers, for example, 1j, -7j or 6j+5. As to verify the variable number is a string, you can readily use the function 'type ().'

A collection of ordered values, which remain unchangeable especially in Python variables, is referred to as a tuple. Python tuples are indicated with round brackets and available in different ways. Some useful in Python variables are access tuple items by index numbers and inside square brackets. Another is tuple remaining unchanged, especially after being created but provides a loop by using the function 'for.' And it readily encompasses both count and index methods of tuple operations.

Types of Data Variables

String

A text string is a type of data variable represented in either String data types or creating a string from a range of type char. The syntax for string data comprises multiple declarations including 'char Str1[15], 'char Str5[8] = "ardiono"; among others. As to declare a string effectively, add null character 'Str3', declare arrays of chars without utilizing in the form of 'Str1', and initialize a given array and leave space for a larger string such as Str6. Strings are usually displayed with doubles quotes despite the several versions of available to construct strings for varying data types.

Char

Char are data types primarily used in variables to store character values with literal values written in single quotes, unlike strings. The values are stores in numbers form, but the specific encoding remains visibly suitable for performing arithmetic. For instance, you can see that it is saved as 'A' +, but it has a value of 66 as the ASCII 'A' value represents 66. Char data types are usually 8 bits, essential for character storage. Characters with larger volumes are stored in bytes. The syntax for this type of variable is 'char var = val'; where 'var' indicates variable name while 'val' represents the value assigned to the variable.

Byte

A byte is a data type necessary for storing 8-bit unsigned numbers that are between 0 to 255 and with a syntax of 'byte var = val;' Like Char data type, 'var' represents variable name while 'val' stands for the value to he assigned that variable. The difference between char and byte is that char stores smaller characters and with a low space volume while byte stores values which are larger.

int

Another type of data type variable is the int, which stores 16-bit value yielding an array of between -32,768 and 32,767, which varies depending on the different programming platforms. Besides, int stores 2's complement math, which is negative numbers, henceforth providing the capability for the variable to store a wide range of values in one reserve. With Python, this type of data variable storage enables transparency in arithmetic operations in an intended manner.

Unsigned int

Unsigned int also referred to, as unsigned integers are data types for storing up to 2 bytes of values but do not include negative numbers. The numbers are all positive with a range of 0 to 65,535 with Duo stores of up to 4 bytes for 32-byte values, which range from 0 to 4,294,967,195. In comparison, unsigned integers comprise positive values and have a much higher bit. However, ints take mostly negative values and have a lower bit hence store chapters with fewer values. The syntax for unsigned int is 'unsigned int var = val;' while an example code being 'unsigned int ledPin = 13;'

Float

Float data types are values with point numbers, that is to say, a number with a decimal point. Floating numbers usually indicate or estimate analog or continuous numbers, as they possess a more advanced resolution compared to integers. The numbers stored may range from the highest of 7.5162306E+38 and the lowest of -3.2095174E+38. Floating-point numbers remain stored in the form of 32 bits taking about 4 bytes per information fed.

Unsigned Long

This is data types of variables with an extended size hence it stores values with larger storages compare to other data types. It stores up to 32 bits for 4 bytes and does not include negative numbers henceforth has a range of 0 to 4,294,967,295. The syntax for the unsigned long data type is 'unsigned long var = val;' essential for storing characters with much larger sizes.

Chapter 5: Inputs, Printing, And Formatting Outputs

Inputs

So far, we've only been writing programs that only use data we have explicitly defined in the script. However, your programs can also take in input from the user and utilize it. Python lets us solicit inputs from the user with a very intuitively named function - the input () function. Writing out the code input () enabless us to prompt the user for information, which we can further manipulate. We can take the user input and save it as a variable, print it straight to the terminal, or do anything else we might like.

When we use the input function, we can pass in a string. The user will see this string as a prompt, and their response to the prompt will be saved as the input value. For instance, if we wanted to query the user for their favorite food, we could write the following:

favorite_food = input ("What is your favorite food? ")

If you ran this code example, you would be prompted for your favorite food. You could save multiple variables this way and print them all at once using the print () function along with print formatting, as we covered earlier. To be clear, the text that you write in the input function is what the user will see as a prompt; it isn't what you are inputting into the system as a value.

When you run the code above, you'll be prompted for an input. After you type in some text and hit the return key, the text you wrote will be stored as the variable favorite_food. The input command can be used along with string formatting to inject variable values into the text that the user will see. For instance, if we had a variable called *user_name* that stored the name of the user, we could structure the input statement like this:

favorite_food = input (" What is ()'s favorite food? "). format (" user name here")

Printing and Formatting Outputs

We've already dealt with the print () function quite a bit, but let's take some time to address it again here and learn a bit more about some of the more advanced things you can do with it.

By now, you've gathered that it prints whatever is in the parentheses to the terminal. In addition, you've learned that you can format the printing of statements with either the modulus operator (%) or the format function (. format ()). However, what should we do if we are in the process of printing a very long message?

In order to prevent a long string from running across the screen, we can use triple quotes that surround our string. Printing with triple quotes allows us to separate our print statements onto multiple lines. For example, we could print like this:

print ("' By using triple quotes we can

divide our print statement onto multiple

lines, making it easier to read. "')

Formatting the print statement like that will give us:

By using triple quotes, we can

divide our print statement onto multiple

lines, making it easier to read.

What if we need to print characters that are equivalent to string formatting instructions? For example, if we ever needed to print out the characters "%s "or "%d ", we would run into trouble. If you recall, these are string formatting commands, and if we try to print these out, the interpreter will interpret them as formatting commands.

Here's a practical example. As mentioned, typing "/t" in our string will put a tab in the middle of our string. Assume we type the following:

print ("We want a \t here, not a tab.")

We'd get back this:

We want a here, not a tab.

By using an escape character, we can tell Python to include the characters that come next as part of the string's value. The escape character we want to use is the "raw string" character, an "r" before the first quote in a string, like this:

print (r"We want a \t here, not a tab.")

So, if we used the raw string, we'd get the format we want back:

We want a \t here, not a tab.

The "raw string" formatter enables you to put any combination of characters you'd like within the string and have it to be considered part of the string's value.

However, what if we did want the tab in the middle of our string? In that case, using special formatting characters in our string is referred to as using "escape characters." "Escaping" a string is a method of reducing the ambiguity in how characters are interpreted. When we use an escape character, we escape the typical method that Python uses to interpret certain characters, and the characters we type are understood to be part of the string's value. The escape primarily used in Python is the backslash (\). The backslash prompts Python to listen for a unique character to follow that will translate to a specific string formatting command.

We already saw that using the "\t" escape character puts a tab in the middle of our string, but there are other escape characters we can use as well.

\n - Starts a new line

\\ - Prints a backslash itself

\" - Prints out a double quote instead of a double quote marking the end   of a string

\' - Like above but prints out a single quote

Input and Formatting Exercise

Let's do another exercise that applies what we've covered in this section. You should try to write a program that does the following:

- Prompts the user for answers to several different questions

- Prints out the answers on different lines using a single print statement

Give this a shot before you look below for an answer to this exercise prompt.

If you've given this a shot, your answer might look something like this:

```
favorite_food = input ("What's your favorite food? :")

favorite_animal = input ("What about your favorite animal? :")

favorite_movie = input ("What's the best movie? :")

print ("Favorite food is: " + favorite_food + "\n" +

    "Favorite animal is: " + favorite_animal + "\n" +

    "Favorite movies is: " + favorite_movie)
```

We've covered a lot of ground in the first quarter of this book. We'll begin covering some more complex topics and concepts. However, before we move on, let's be sure that we've got the basics down. You won't learn the new concepts unless you are familiar with what we've covered so far, so for that reason, let's do a quick review of what we've learned so far:

Variables - Variables are representations of values. They contain the value and allow the value to be manipulated without having to write it out every time. Variables must contain only letters, numbers, or underscores. In addition, the first character in a variable cannot be a number, and the variable name must not be one of Python's reserved keywords.

Operators - Operators are symbols which are used to manipulate data. The assignment operator (=) is used to store values in variables. Other operators in Python include: the addition operator (+), the subtraction operator (-), the multiplication operator (*), the division operator (/), the floor division operator (//), the modulus operator (%), and the exponent operator (**). The mathematical operators can be combined with the assignment operator. (Ex. +=, -=, *=).

Strings - Strings are text data, declared by wrapping text in single or double-quotes. There are two methods of formatting strings; with the modulus operator or the. format () command. The "s," "d," and "f" modifiers are used to specify the placement of strings, integers, and floats.

Integers - Integers are whole numbers, numbers that possess no decimal points or fractions. Integers can be stored in variables simply by using the assignment operator.

Floats - Floats are numbers that possess decimal parts. The method of creating a float in Python is the same as declaring an integer, just choose a name for the variable and then use the assignment operator.

Type Casting - Type casting allows you to convert one data type to another if the conversion is feasible (non-numerical strings cannot be converted into integers or floats). You can use the following functions to convert data types: int (), float (), and str ().

Lists - Lists are just collections of data, and they can be declared with brackets and commas separating the values within the brackets. Empty lists can also be created. List items can be accessed by specifying the position of the desired item. The append () function is used to add an item to a list, while the del command and remove () function can be used to remove items from a list.

List Slicing - List slicing is a method of selecting values from a list. The item at the first index is included, but the item at the second index isn't. A third value, a stepper value, can also be used to slice the list, skipping through the array at a rate specified by the value. (Ex. - numbers [0:9:2])

Tuples - Tuples are like lists, but they are immutable; unlike lists, their contents cannot be modified once they are created. When a list is created, parentheses are used instead of brackets.

Dictionaries - Dictionaries stored data in key/value pairs. When a dictionary is declared, the data and the key that will point to the data must be specified, and the key-value pairs must be unique. The syntax for creating a key in Python is curly braces containing the key on the left side and the value on the right side, separated by a colon.

Inputs - The input () function gets an input from the user. A string is passed into the parenthesis, which the user will see when they are prompted to enter a string or numerical value.

Formatting Printing - Triple quotes allows us to separate our print statement onto multiple lines. Escape characters are used to specify that certain formatting characters, like "\n" and "\t," should be included in a string's value. Meanwhile, the "raw string" command, "r," can be used to include all the characters within the quotes.

Chapter 6: Mathematical Notation, Basic Terminology, and Building Machine Learning Systems

Mathematical Notation for Machine Learning

In your process of machine learning, you will realize that mathematical nomenclature and notations go hand in hand throughout your project. There is a variety of signs, symbols, values, and variables used in the course of mathematics to describe whatever algorithms you may be trying to accomplish.

You will find yourself using some of the mathematical notations within this field of model development. You will find that values that deal with data and the process of learning or memory formation will always take precedence. Therefore, the following six examples are the most commonly used notations. Each of these notations has a description for which its algorithm explains:

1. Algebra

To indicate a change or difference: Delta

To give the total summation of all values: Summation

To describe a nested function: Composite function

To indicate Euler's number and Epsilon where necessary

To describe the product of all values: Capital pi

2. Calculus

To describe a particular gradient: Nabla

To describe the first derivative: Derivative

To describe the second derivative: Second derivative

To describe a function value as x approaches zero: Limit

3. Linear Algebra

To describe capitalized variables are matrices: Matrix

To describe matrix transpose: Transpose

To describe a matrix or vector: Brackets

To describe a dot product: Dot

To describe a Hadamard product: Hadamard

To describe a vector: Vector

To describe a vector of magnitude 1: Unit vector

4. Probability

The probability of an event: Probability

5. Set theory

To describe a list of distinct elements: Set

6. Statistics

To describe the median value of variable x: Median

To describe the correlation between variables X and Y: Correlation

To describe the standard deviation of a sample set: Sample standard deviation

To describe the population standard deviation: Standard deviation

To describe the variance of a subset of a population: Sample variance

To describe the variance of a population value: Population variance

To describe the mean of a subset of a population: Sample mean

To describe the mean of population values: Population means

Terminologies Used for Machine Learning

The following terminologies are what you will encounter most often during machine learning. You may be getting into machine learning for professional purposes or even as an artificial intelligence (AI) enthusiast. Anyway, whatever your reasons, the following are categories and subcategories of terminologies that you will need to know and probably understand to get along with your colleagues. In this section, you will get to see the significant picture explanation and then delve into the subcategories. Here are machine-learning terms that you need to know:

1. Natural language processing (NLP)

Natural language is what you as a human, use, i.e., human language. By definition, NLP is a way of machine learning where the machine learns your human form of communication. NLP is the standard base for all if not most machine languages that allow your device to make use of human (natural) language. This NLP ability enables your machine to hear your natural (human) input, understand it, execute it then give a data output. The device can realize humans and interact appropriately or as close to appropriate as possible.

There are five primary stages in NLP: machine translation, information retrieval, sentiment analysis, information extraction, and finally question answering. It begins with the human query which straight-up leads to machine translation and then through all the four other processes and finally ending up in question explaining itself. You can now break down these five stages into subcategories as suggested earlier:

Text classification and ranking - This step is a filtering mechanism that determines the class of importance based on relevance algorithms that filter out unwanted stuff such as spam or junk mail. It filters out what needs precedence and the order of execution up to the final task.

Sentiment analysis - This analysis predicts the emotional reaction of a human towards the feedback provided by the machine. Customer relations and satisfaction are factors that may benefit from sentiment analysis.

Document summarization - As the phrase suggests, this is a means of developing short and precise definitions of complex and complicated descriptions. The overall purpose is to make it easy to understand.

Named-Entity Recognition (NER) - This activity involves getting structured and identifiable data from an unstructured set of words. The machine learning process learns to identify the most appropriate keywords, applies those words to the context of the speech, and tries to come up with the most appropriate response. Keywords are things like company name, employee name, calendar date, and time.

Speech recognition - An example of this mechanism can easily be appliances such as Alexa. The machine learns to associate the spoken text to the speech originator. The device can identify audio signals from human speech and vocal sources.

It understands Natural language and generation - As opposed to Named-Entity Recognition; these two concepts deal with human to computer and vice versa conversions. Natural language understanding allows the machine to convert and interpret the human form of spoken text into a coherent set of understandable computer format. On the other hand, natural language generation does the reverse function, i.e., transforming the incorrect computer format to the human audio format that is understandable by the human ear.

Machine translation - This action is an automated system of converting one written human language into another human language. Conversion enables people from different ethnic backgrounds and different styles to understand each other. An artificial intelligence entity that has gone through the process of machine learning carries out this job.

2. Dataset

A dataset is a range of variables that you can use to test the viability and progress of your machine learning. Data is an essential component of your machine learning progress. It gives results that are indicative of your development and areas that need adjustments and tweaking for fine-tuning specific factors. There are three types of datasets:

Training data - As the name suggests, training data is used to predict patterns by letting the model learn via deduction. Due to the enormity of factors to be trained on, yes, there will be factors that are more important than others are. These features get a training priority. Your machine-learning model will use the more prominent features to predict the most appropriate patterns required. Over time, your model will learn through training.

Validation data - This set is the data that is used to micro tune the small tiny aspects of the different models that are at the completion phase. Validation testing is not a training phase; it is a final comparison phase. The data obtained from your validation is used to choose your final model. You get to validate the various aspects of the models under comparison and then make a final decision based on this validation data.

Test data - Once you have decided on your final model, test data is a stage that will give you vital information on how the model will handle in real life. The test data will be carried out using an utterly different set of parameters from the ones used during both training and validation. Having the model go through this kind of test data will give you an indication of how your model will handle the types of other types of inputs. You will get answers to questions such as how will the fail-safe mechanism react. Will the fail-safe even come online in the first place?

3. Computer vision

Computer vision is responsible for the tools providing a high-level analysis of image and video data. Challenges that you should look out for in computer vision are:

Image classification - This training allows the model to identify and learn what various images and pictorial representations are. The model needs to retain a memory of a familiar-looking image to maintain mind and identify the correct image even with minor alterations such as color changes.

Object detection - Unlike image classification, which detects whether there is an image in your model field of view, object detection allows it to identify objects. Object identification enables the model to take a large set of data and then frames them to detect a pattern recognition. It is akin to facial recognition since it looks for patterns within a given field of view.

Image segmentation - The model will associate a specific image or video pixel with a previously encountered pixel. This association depends on the concept of a most likely scenario based on the frequency of association between a particular pixel and a corresponding specific predetermined set.

Saliency detection - In this case, it will involve that you train and get your model accustomed to increase its visibility. For instance, advertisements are best at locations with higher human traffic. Hence, your model will learn to place itself at positions of maximum social visibility. This computer vision feature will naturally attract human attention and curiosity.

4. Supervised learning

You achieve supervised learning by having the models teach themselves by using targeted examples. If you wanted to show the models how to recognize a given task, then you would label the dataset for that particular supervised task. You will then present the model with the set of labeled examples and monitor its learning through supervision.

The models get to learn themselves through constant exposure to the correct patterns. You want to promote brand awareness; you could apply supervised learning where the model leans by using the product example and mastering its art of advertisement.

5. Unsupervised learning

This learning style is the opposite of supervised learning. In this case, your models learn through observations. There is no supervision involved, and the datasets are not labeled; hence, there is no correct base value as learned from the supervised method.

Here, through constant observations, your models will get to determine their right truths. Unsupervised models most often learn through associations between different structures and elemental characteristics common to the datasets. Since unsupervised learning deals with similar groups of related datasets, they are useful in clustering.

6. Reinforcement learning

Reinforcement learning teaches your model to strive for the best result always. In addition to only performing its assigned tasks correctly, the model gets rewarded with a treat. This learning technique is a form of encouragement to your model to always deliver the correct action and perform it well or to the best of its ability. After some time, your model will learn to expect a present or favor, and therefore, the model will always strive for the best outcome.

This example is a form of positive reinforcement. It rewards good behavior. However, there is another type of support called negative reinforcement. Negative reinforcement aims to punish or discourage bad behavior. The model gets reprimanded in cases where the supervisor did not meet the expected standards. The model learns as well that lousy behavior attracts penalties, and it will always strive to do good continually.

Chapter 7: Lists and Sets Python

Lists

We create a list in Python by placing items called elements inside square brackets separated by commas. The items in a list can be of a mixed data type.

Start IDLE.

Navigate to the File menu and click New Window.

Type the following:

list_mine= [] #empty list list_mine= [2,5,8] #list of integers

list_mine= [5," Happy", 5.2] #list having mixed data types

Practice Exercise

Write a program that captures the following in a list: "Best", 26,89,3.9

Nested Lists

A nested list is a list as an item in another list.

Example

Start IDLE.

Navigate to the File menu and click New Window.

Type the following: list_mine= ["carrot", [9, 3, 6], ['g']]

Practice Exercise

Write a nested for the following elements: [36,2,1],"
Writer",'t', [3.0, 2.5]

Accessing Elements from a List

In programming and in Python specifically, the first time is always indexed zero. For a list of five items, we will access them from index0 to index4. Failure to access the items in a list in this manner will create index error. The index is always an integer as using other number types will create a type error. For nested lists, they are accessed via nested indexing.

Example

Start IDLE.

Navigate to the File menu and click New Window.

Type the following:

list_mine=['b','e','s','t'] print(list_mine[0])   #the output will be b print(list_mine[2])   #the output will be s print(list_mine[3])   #the output will be t

Practice Exercise Given the following list: your_collection=['t','k','v','w','z','n','f']

✓   Write a Python program to display the second item in the list

✓   Write a Python program to display the sixth item in the last ✓   Write a Python program to display the last item in the list.

Nested List Indexing

Start IDLE.

Navigate to the File menu and click New Window.

Type the following:

nested_list= ["Best', [4,7,2,9]]

print (nested_list [0][1]

Python Negative Indexing

For its sequences, Python allows negative indexing. The last item on the list is index-1, index -2 is the second last item, and so on.

Start IDLE.

Navigate to the File menu and click New Window.

Type the following:

list_mine=['c','h','a','n','g','e','s'] print (list_mine [-1]) #Output is s print (list_mine [-4]) ##Output is n

Slicing Lists in Python

Slicing operator (full colon) is used to access a range of elements in a list.

Example

Start IDLE.

Navigate to the File menu and click New Window.

Type the following:

list_mine=['c','h','a','n','g','e','s']

print (list_mine [3:5]) #Picking elements from the 4 to the sixth

Example

Picking elements from start to the fifth Start IDLE.

Navigate to the File menu and click New Window.

Type the following: print (list_mine [: -6])

Example

Picking the third element to the last.

print (list_mine [2:])

Practice Exercise

Given class_names= ['John', 'Kelly', 'Yvonne', 'Una','Lovy','Pius', 'Tracy']

✓　　　　　Write a python program using a slice operator to display from the second students and the rest.

✓　　　　　Write a python program using a slice operator to display the first student to the third using a negative indexing feature.

✓　　　　　Write a python program using a slice operator to display the fourth and fifth students only.

Manipulating Elements in a List using the assignment operator

Items in a list can be changed meaning lists are mutable.

Start IDLE.

Navigate to the File menu and click New Window.

Type the following: list_yours= [4,8,5,2,1] list_yours [1] =6

print(list_yours) #The output will be [4,6,5,2,1]

Changing a range of items in a list

Start IDLE.

Navigate to the File menu and click New Window.

Type the following: list_yours [0:3] = [12,11,10] #Will change first item to fourth item in the list print(list_yours) #Output will be: [12,11,10,1]

Appending/Extending items in the List

The append () method allows extending the items on the list. The extend () can also be used.

Example

Start IDLE.

Navigate to the File menu and click New Window.

Type the following: list_yours= [4, 6, 5] list_yours. append (3)

print(list_yours) #The output will be [4,6,5, 3]

Example

Start IDLE.

Navigate to the File menu and click New Window.

Type the following: list_yours= [4,6,5] list_yours. extend ([13,7,9])

print(list_yours) #The output will be [4,6,5,13,7,9]

The plus operator (+) can also be used to combine two lists. The * operator can be used to iterate a list a given number of times.

Example

Start IDLE.

Navigate to the File menu and click New Window.

Type the following: list_yours= [4,6,5]

print (list_yours+ [13,7,9]) # Output: [4, 6, 5,13,7,9]

print(['happy'] *4) #Output: ["happy"," happy", "happy","
happy"]

Removing or Deleting Items from a List

The keyword del is used to delete elements or the entire list
in Python.

Example

Start IDLE.

Navigate to the File menu and click New Window.

Type the following:

list_mine=['t','r','o','g','r','a','m'] del list_mine [1]
print(list_mine) #t, o, g, r, a, m

Deleting Multiple Elements

Example

Start IDLE.

Navigate to the File menu and click New Window.

Type the following: del list_mine [0:3]

Example

print(list_mine) #a, m

Delete Entire List Start IDLE.

Navigate to the File menu and click New Window.

Type the following:

delete list_mine

print(list_mine) #will generate an error of lost not found

The remove () method or pop () method can be used to remove the specified item. The pop () method will remove and return the last item if the index is not given and helps implement lists as stacks. The clear () method is used to empty a list.

Start IDLE.

Navigate to the File menu and click New Window.

Type the following: list_mine=['t','k','b','d','w','q','v'] list_mine.remove('t') print(list_mine)   #output will be ['t','k','b','d','w','q','v'] print(list_mine.pop(1))   #output will be 'k' print(list_mine.pop())   #output will be 'v'

Practice Exercise

Given list_yours=['K','N','O','C','K','E','D']

✓   Pop the third item in the list, save the program as list1.

✓ Remove the fourth item using remove () method and save the program as list2

✓ Delete the second item in the list and save the program as list3.

✓ Pop the list without specifying an index and save the program as list4.

Using Empty List to Delete an Entire or Specific Elements

Start IDLE.

Navigate to the File menu and click New Window.

Type the following: list_mine=['t','k','b','d','w','q','v']
list_mine= [1:2] = []

print(list_mine) #Output will be ['t','w','q','v']

Practice Exercise

➢ Use list access methods to display the following items in reversed order list_yours= [4,9,2,1,6,7]

➢ Use list access method to count the elements in a.

➢ Use list access method to sort the items in a. in an ascending order/default.

Summary

Lists store an ordered collection of items which can be of different types. The list defined above has items that are all of the same type (int), but all the items of a list do not need to be of the same type as you can see below.

Define a list

heterogenousElements = [3, True, 'Michael', 2.0]

Sets

The attributes of a set are that it contains unique elements, the items are not ordered, and the elements are not changeable. The set itself can be changed.

Creating a set

Example

Start IDLE.

Navigate to the File menu and click New Window.

Type the following: set_mine= {5,6,7} print(set_mine)

set_yours= {2.1," Great", (7,8,9)} print(set_mine)

Creating a Set from a List

Example

Start IDLE.

Navigate to the File menu and click New Window.

Type the following: set_mine=set ([5,6,7,5])
print(set_mine) Practice Exercise Start IDLE.

Navigate to the File menu and click New Window.

Type the following:

Correct and create a set in Python given the following set,
trial_set= {1,1,2,3,1,5,8,9}

Note

The {} will create a dictionary that is empty in Python.
There is no need to index sets since they are ordered.

Adding elements to a set for multiple members we use the
update () method.

For a single addition of a single element to a set, we use the
add () method. Duplicates should be avoided when
handling sets.

Example

Start IDLE.

Navigate to the File menu and click New Window.

Type the following: your_set={6,7} print(your_set)
your_set.add(4) print(your_set) your_set.update([9,10,13])
print(your_set) your_set.update([23, 37],{11,16,18})
print(your_set)

Removing Elements from a Set

The methods discard (o and remove () are used to purge an item from a set.

Example

Start IDLE.

Navigate to the File menu and click New Window.

Type the following: set_mine= {7,2,3,4,1} print(set_mine) set_mine. discard (2) print(set_mine) #Output will be {7,3,4,1} set_mine. remove (1)

print(set_mine) #Output will be {7,3,4}

Using the pop () Method to Remove an Item from a Set

Since sets are unordered, the order of popping items is arbitrary.

It is also possible to remove all items in a set using the clear () method in Python.

Start IDLE.

Navigate to the File menu and click New Window.

Type the following: your_set=set("Today") print(your_set) print (your_set.pop ()) your_set.pop () print(your_set) your_set. clear () print(your_set)

Set Operations in Python

We use sets to compute difference, intersection, and union of sets.

Example

Start IDLE.

Navigate to the File menu and click New Window.

Type the following:

C= {5,6,7,8,9,11} D= {6,9,11,13,15}

Set Union

A union of sets C and D will contain both sets' elements.

In Python the| operator generates a union of sets. The union () will also generate a union of sets.

Example

Start IDLE.

Navigate to the File menu and click New Window.

Type the following:

C= {5,6,7,8,9,11} D= {6,9,11,13,15}

print(C|D)   #Output: {5,6,7,8,9,11,13,15}

Example 2

Using the union () Start IDLE.

Navigate to the File menu and click New Window.

Type the following:

C= {5,6,7,8,9,11} D= {6,9,11,13,15}

print (D. union(C)) #Output: {5,6,7,8,9,11,13,15}

Practice Exercise

Rewrite the following into a set and find the set union.

A= {1,1,2,3,4,4,5,12,14,15}

D= {2,3,3,7,8,9,12,15}

Set Intersection

A and D refer to a new item set that is shared by both sets. The & operator is used to perform intersection. The intersection () function can also be used to intersect sets.

Example

Start IDLE.

Navigate to the File menu and click New Window.

Type the following:

A = {11, 12, 13, 14, 15}

D= {14, 15,16, 17, 18}

Print(A&D)   #Will display {14,15}

Using intersection ()

Example

Start IDLE.

Navigate to the File menu and click New Window.

Type the following:

A = {11, 12, 13, 14, 15}

D= {14, 15,16, 17, 18}

    A. intersection(D)

Chapter 8: Conditions Statements

Computing numbers and processing text are two basic functionalities by which a program instructs a computer. An advanced or complex computer program has the capability to change its program flow. That is usually done by allowing it to make choices and decisions through conditional statements.

Condition statements are one of a few elements that control and direct your program's flow. Other common elements that can affect program flow are functions and loops.

A program with a neat and efficient program flow is like a create-your-own-adventure book. The progressions, outcomes, or results of your program depend on your user input and runtime environment.

For example, say that your computer program involves talking about cigarette consumption and vaping. You would not want minors to access the program to prevent any legal issues.

A simple way to prevent a minor from accessing your program is to ask the user his age. This information is then passed on to a common functionality within your program that decides if the age of the user is acceptable or not.

Programs and websites usually do this by asking for the user's birthday. That being said, the below example will only process the input age of the user for simplicity's sake.

```
>>> user Age = 12
>>> if (userAge < 18):
    print ("You are not allowed to access this program.")
  else:
    print ("You can access this program.")
You are not allowed to access this program.
>>> _
```

Here is the same code with the user's age set above 18.

```
>>> userAge = 19
>>> if (userAge < 18):
    print ("You are not allowed to access this program.")
  else:
    print ("You can access this program.")
You can access this program.
>>> _
```

The if and else operators are used to create condition statements. Condition statements have three parts. The conditional keyword, the Boolean value from a literal, variable, or expression, and the statements to execute.

In the above example, the keywords *if* and *else* were used to control the program's flow. The program checks if the variable *userAge* contains a value less than 18. If it does, a warning message is displayed. Otherwise, the program will display a welcome message.

The example used the comparison operator less than (<). It basically checks the values on either side of the operator symbol. If the value of the operand on the left side of the operator symbol was less than that on the right side, it will return True. Otherwise, if the value of the operand on the left side of the operator symbol was equal or greater than the value on the right side, it will return False.

"if" statements

The if keyword needs a literal, variable, or expression that returns a Boolean value, which can be True or False. Remember these two things:

1. If the value of the element next to the if keyword is equal to True, the program will process the statements within the if block.

2. If the value of the element next to the if keyword is equal to False, the program will skip or ignore the statements within the if block.

Else Statements

Else statements are used in conjunction with "if" statements. They are used to perform alternative statements if the preceding "if" statement returns False.

In the previous example, if the userAge is equal or greater than 18, the expression in the "if" statement will return False. And since the expression returns False on the "if" statement, the statements in the else statement will be executed.

On the other hand, if the userAge is less than 18, the expression in the "if" statement will return True. When that happens, the statements within the "if" statement will be executed while those in the else statement will be ignored.

Mind you, an else statement has to be preceded by an "if" statement. If there is none, the program will return an error. Also, you can put an else statement after another else statement as long as it precedes an "if" statement.

In summary:

1. If the "if" statement returns True, the program will skip the else statement that follows.

2. If the "if" statement returns False, the program will process the else statement code block.

Code Blocks

Just to jog your memory, code blocks are simply groups of statements or declarations that follow *if* and *else* statements.

Creating code blocks is an excellent way to manage your code and make it efficient. You will mostly be working with statements and scenarios that will keep you working on code blocks.

Aside from that, you will learn about the variable scope as you progress. For now, you will mostly be creating code blocks "for" loops.

Loops are an essential part of programming. Every program that you use and see use loops.

Loops are blocks of statements that are executed repeatedly until a condition is met. It also starts when a condition is satisfied.

By the way, did you know that your monitor refreshes the image itself 60 times a second? Refresh means displaying a new image. The computer itself has a looping program that creates a new image on the screen.

You may not create a program with a complex loop to handle the display, but you will definitely use one in one of your programs. A good example is a small snippet of a program that requires the user to login using a password.

For example:

```
>>> password = "secret"

>>> user Input = ""

>>> while (userInput! = password):
    userInput = input ()
```

This example will ask for a user input. On the text cursor, you need to type the password and then press the Enter key. The program will keep on asking for a user input until you type the word secret.

While

Loops are easy to code. All you need is the correct keyword, a conditional value, and statements you want to execute repeatedly.

One of the keywords that you can use to loop is *while*. While is like an "if" statement. If its condition is met or returns True, it will start the loop. Once the program executes the last statement in the code block, it will recheck the while statement and condition again. If the condition still returns True, the code block will be executed again. If the condition returns False, the code block will be ignored, and the program will execute the next line of code. For example

```
>>> i = 1
>>> while i < 6:
     print(i)
       i += 1

1

2

3

4

5
>>> _
```

For Loop

While the while loop statement loops until the condition returns false, the "for" loop statement will loop at a set number of times depending on a string, tuple, or list. For example:

>>> carBrands = ["Toyota", "Volvo", "Mitsubishi", "Volkswagen"]

>>> for brands in carBrands:

    print(brands)

Toyota

Volvo

Mitsubishi

Volkswagen

>>> _

Break

Break is a keyword that stops a loop. Here is one of the previous examples combined with break.

For example:

>>> password = "secret"

>>> userInput = ""

>>> while (userInput! = password):

    userInput = input ()

```
    break

    print ("This will not get printed.")
```

Wrongpassword

```
>>> _
```

As you can see here, the while loop did not execute the print keyword and did not loop again after an input was provided since the break keyword came after the input assignment.

The break keyword allows you to have better control of your loops. For example, if you want to loop a code block in a set amount of times without using sequences, you can use while and break.

```
>>> x = 0
>>> while (True):
    x += 1
    print(x)
    if (x == 5):
        break
1
2
3
```

4

5

>>> _

Using a counter, variable x (any variable will do of course) with an integer that increments every loop in this case, condition and break is common practice in programming. In most programming languages, counters are even integrated in loop statements. Here is a "for" loop with a counter in JavaScript.

```
for (i = 0; i < 10; i++) {

    alert(i);

}
```

This script will loop for ten times. On one line, the counter variable is declared, assigned an initial value, a conditional expression was set, and the increments for the counter are already coded.

Infinite Loop

You should be always aware of the greatest problem with coding loops: infinity loops. Infinity loops are loops that never stop. And since they never stop, they can easily make your program become unresponsive, crash, or hog all your computer's resources. Here is an example similar with the previous one but without the counter and the usage of break.

```
>>> while (True):
        print ("This will never end until you close the
program")
```

This will never end until you close the program

This will never end until you close the program

This will never end until you close the program

Whenever possible, always include a counter and break statement in your loops. Doing this will prevent your program from having infinite loops.

Continue

The continue keyword is like a soft version of break. Instead of breaking out from the whole loop, "continue" just breaks away from one loop and directly goes back to the loop statement. For example:

```
>>> password = "secret"
>>> userInput = ""
>>> while (userInput! = password):
        userInput = input ()
```

```
    continue

    print ("This will not get printed.")

Wrongpassword

Test

secret

>>> _
```

When this example was used on the break keyword, the program only asks for user input once regardless of anything you enter and it ends the loop if you enter anything. This version, on the other hand, will still persist on asking input until you put the right password. However, it will always skip on the print statement and always go back directly to the while statement.

Here is a practical application to make it easier to know the purpose of the continue statement.

```
>>> carBrands = ["Toyota", "Volvo", "Mitsubishi", "Volkswagen"]
>>> for brands in carBrands:
    if (brands == "Volvo"):

        continue

    print ("I have a " + brands)
```

I have a Toyota

I have a Mitsubishi

I have a Volkswagen

>>> _

When you are parsing or looping a sequence, there are items that you do not want to process. You can skip the ones you do not want to process by using a continue statement. In the above example, the program did not print "I have a Volvo", because it hit *continue* when a Volvo was selected. This caused it to go back and process the next car brand in the list.

Practice Exercise

For this chapter, create a choose-your-adventure program. The program should provide users with two options. It must also have at least five choices and have at least two different endings.

You must also use dictionaries to create dialogues.

Here is an example:

creepometer = 1

prompt = "\nType 1 or 2 then press enter...\n\n: :> "

clearScreen = ("\n" * 25)

scenario = [

"You see your crush at the other side of the road on your way to school.",

"You notice that her handkerchief fell on the ground.",

"You heard a ring. She reached on to her pocket to get her phone and stopped.",

"Both of you reached the pedestrian crossing, but its currently red light.",

"You got her attention now and you instinctively grabbed your phone."

]

choice1 = [

"Follow her using your eyes and cross when you reach the intersection.",

"Pick it up and give it to her.",

"Walk pass her.",

"Smile and wave at her.",

"Ask for her number."

Chapter 9: Iteration

The term iteration in programming refers to the repetition of lines of code. It is a useful concept in programming that helps determine solutions to problems. Iteration and conditional execution are the reference for algorithm development.

While Statement

The following program counts to five, and prints a number on every output line.

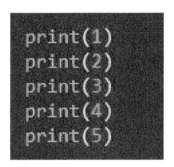

```
print(1)
print(2)
print(3)
print(4)
print(5)
```

Well, how can you write a code that can count to 10,000? Are you going to copy-paste and change the 10, 000 printing statements? You can but that is going to be tiresome. But counting is a common thing and computers count large values. So, there must be an efficient way to do so. What you need to do is to print the value of a variable and start to increment the variable, and repeat the process until you get 10,000. This process of implementing the same code, again and again, is known as looping. In Python, there are two unique statements, while and for, that support iteration.

Here is a program that uses while statement to count to five:

```
count = 1 # Initialize counter
while count <= 5: # Should we continue?
print(count) # Display counter, then
count += 1 # Increment counter
```

The while statement used in this particular program will repeatedly output the variable count. The program then implements this block of statement five times:

```
print(count)
count += 1
```

After every display of the count variable, the program increases it by one. Finally, after five repetitions, the condition will not be true, and the block of code is not executed anymore.

This line `while count <= 5:` is the opening of the while statement. The expression that follows the while keyword is the condition that determines whether the block is executed. As long as the result of the condition is true, the program will continue to run the code block over and over. But when the condition becomes false, the loop terminates. Also, if the condition is evaluated as false at the start, the program cannot implement the code block inside the body of the loop.

The general syntax of the while statement is:

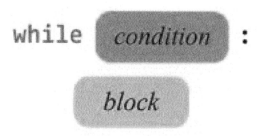

```
while condition :
    block
```

The word while is a Python reserved word that starts the statement.

The condition shows whether the body will be executed or not. A colon (:) has to come after the condition.

A block is made up of one or more statements that should be implemented if the condition is found to be true. All statements that make up the block must be indented one level deeper than the first line of the while statement. Technically, the block belongs to the while statement.

The while statement can resemble the if statements and thus new programmers may confuse the two. Sometimes, they may type if when they wanted to use while. Often, the uniqueness of the two statements shows the problem instantly. But in some nested and advanced logic, this error can be hard to notice.

The running program evaluates the condition before running the while block and then confirms the condition after running the while block. If the condition remains true, the program will continuously run the code in the while block. If initially, the condition is true, the program will run the block iteratively until when the condition is false. This is the point when the loop exits from execution.

Below is a program that will count from zero as long as the user wants it to do.

```python
# Counts up from zero. The user continues the count by entering
# 'Y'. The user discontinues the count by entering 'N'.
count = 0 # The current count
entry = 'Y' # Count to begin with
while entry != 'N' and entry != 'n':
# Print the current value of count
print(count)
entry = input('Please enter "Y" to continue or "N" to quit: ')
if entry == 'Y' or entry == 'y':
count += 1 # Keep counting
# Check for "bad" entry
elif entry != 'N' and entry != 'n':
print('"' + entry + '" is not a valid choice')
# else must be 'N' or 'n'
```

Here is another program that will let the user type different non-negative integers. If the user types a negative value, the program stops to accept inputs and outputs the total of all nonnegative values. In case a negative number is the first entry, the sum will be zero.

```python
# Allow the user to enter a sequence of nonnegative
# integers. The user ends the list with a negative
# integer. At the end the sum of the nonnegative
# numbers entered is displayed. The program prints
# zero if the user provides no nonnegative numbers.
entry = 0 # Ensure the loop is entered
sum = 0 # Initialize sum
# Request input from the user
print("Enter numbers to sum, negative number ends list:")
while entry >= 0: # A negative number exits the loop
entry = int(input()) # Get the value
if entry >= 0: # Is number nonnegative?
sum += entry # Only add it if it is nonnegative
print("Sum =", sum) # Display the sum
```

Let us explore the details of this program:

First, the program uses two variables, sum and entry.

- Entry

At the start, you will initialize the entry to zero because we want the condition entry >=0 of the while statement to be true. Failure to initialize the variable entry, the program will generate a run-time error when it tries to compare entry to zero in the while condition. The variable entry stores the number typed by the user. The value of the variable entry changes every time inside the loop.

- Sum

This variable is one that stores the total of each number entered by the user. For this particular variable, it is initialized to zero in the start because a value of zero shows that it has not evaluated anything. If you don't initialize the variable sum, the program will also generate a run-time error when it tries to apply the +- operator to change the variable. Inside the loop, you can constantly add the user's input values to sum. When the loop completes, the variable sum will feature the total of all nonnegative values typed by the user.

The initialization of the entry to zero plus the condition entry >= 0 of the whiles ensures that the program will run the body of the while loop only once. The if statement confirms that the program won't add a negative entry to the sum.

When a user types a negative value, the running program may not update the sum variable and the condition of the while will not be true. The loop exits and the program implements the print statement.

This program doesn't store the number of values typed. But it adds the values entered in the variable sum.

```
print("Help! My computer doesn't work!")
done = False # Not done initially
while not done:
print("Does the computer make any sounds (fans, etc.) ")
choice = input("or show any lights? (y/n):")
# The troubleshooting control logic
if choice == 'n': # The computer does not have power
choice = input("Is it plugged in? (y/n):")
if choice == 'n': # It is not plugged in, plug it in
print("Plug it in.")
else: # It is plugged in
choice = input("Is the switch in the \"on\" position? (y/n):")
if choice == 'n': # The switch is off, turn it on!
print("Turn it on.")
else: # The switch is on
choice = input("Does the computer have a fuse? (y/n):")
if choice == 'n': # No fuse
choice = input("Is the outlet OK? (y/n):")
if choice == 'n': # Fix outlet
print("Check the outlet's circuit ")
print("breaker or fuse. Move to a")
print("new outlet, if necessary. ")
else: # Beats me!
print("Please consult a service technician.")
done = True # Nothing else I can do
else: # Check fuse
print("Check the fuse. Replace if ")
print("necessary.")
else: # The computer has power
print("Please consult a service technician.")
done = True # Nothing else I can do
```

A while block occupies a huge percent of this program. The program has a Boolean variable done that regulates the loop. The loop will continue to run as long as done is false. The name of this Boolean variable called a flag. Now, when the flag is raised, the value is true, if not, the value is false.

Don't forget the not done is the opposite of the variable done.

Definite and Indefinite Loops

Let us look at the following code:

```
n = 1
while n <= 10:
print(n)
n += 1
```

We examine this code and establish the correct number of iterations inside the loop. This type of loop is referred to as a definite loop because we can accurately tell the number of times the loop repeats.

Now, take a look at the following code:

```
n = 1
stop = int(input())
while n <= stop:
print(n)
n += 1
```

In this code, it is hard to establish the number of times it will loop. The number of repetitions relies on the input entered by the user. But it is possible to know the number of repetitions the while loop will make at the point of execution after entering the user's input before the next execution begins.

For that reason, the loop is said to be a definite loop.

Now compare the previous programs with this one:

```
done = False # Enter the loop at least once
while not done:
entry = int(input()) # Get value from user
if entry == 999: # Did user provide the magic number?
done = True # If so, get out
else:
print(entry) # If not, print it and continue
```

For this program, you cannot tell at any point inside the loop's execution the number of times the iterations can run. The value 999 is known before and after the loop but the value of the entry can be anything the user inputs. The user can decide to input 0 or even 999 and end it. The while statement in this program is a great example of an indefinite loop.

So, the while statement is perfect for indefinite loops. While these examples have applied the while statements to demonstrate definite loops, Python has a better option for definite loops. That is none other than the for statement.

The for Statement

The while loop is perfect for indefinite loops. This has been demonstrated in the previous programs, where it is impossible to tell the number of times the while loop will run. Previously, the while loop was used to run a definite loop such as:

```
n = 1
while n <= 10:
    print(n)
    n += 1
```

In the following code snippet, the print statement will only run 10 times. This code demands three important parts to control the loop:

- Initialization

- Check

- Update

Python language has an efficient method to demonstrate a definite loop. The *for* statement repeats over a series of values. One method to demonstrate a series is to use a tuple. For example:

```
for n in 1, 2, 3, 4, 5, 6, 7, 8, 9, 10:
    print(n)
```

This code works the same way as the while loop is shown earlier. In this example, the print statement runs 10 times. The code will print first 1, then 2, and so forth. The last value it prints is 10.

It is always tedious to display all elements of a tuple. Imagine going over all the integers from 1 to 1, 000, and outputting all the elements of the tuple in writing. That would be impractical. Fortunately, Python has an efficient means of displaying a series of integers that assume a consistent pattern.

This code applies the range expression to output integers between 1-10.

```python
for n in range(1, 11):
print(n)
```

The range expression (1,11) develops a range object that will let the for loop to allocate the variable n the values 1, 2, ...10.

The line of code in this code snippet is interpreted as "for every integer n in the range 1 ≤ n < 11." In the first execution of the loop, the value of n is 1 inside the block. In the next iteration of the loop, the value of n is 2. The value of n increases by one for each loop. The code inside the block will apply the value of n until it hits 10. The general format for the range expression goes as follows:

range(*begin*, *end*, *step*)

From the general syntax:

- Begin represents the leading value in the range; when it is deleted, the default value becomes 0.

- The end value is one value after the last value. This value is necessary, and should not be deleted.

- Step represents the interval of increase or decrease. The default value for step is 1 if it is deleted.

All the values for begin, step, and end must be integer expressions. Floating-point expressions and other types aren't allowed. The arguments that feature inside the range expression can be literal numbers such as 10, or even variables like m, n, and some complex integer expressions.

One thing good about the range expression is the flexibility it brings. For example:

```
for n in range(21, 0, -3):
print(n, end=' ')

output

21 18 15 12 9 6 3
```

This means that you can use the range to display a variety of sequences.

For range expressions that have a single argument like range(y), the y is the end of the range, while 0 is the beginning value, and then 1 the step value.

For expressions carrying two arguments like range (m, n), m is the begin value, while y is the end of the range. The step value becomes 1.

For expressions that have three arguments like range (m, n, y), m is the begin value, n is the end, and y is the step value.

When it comes to a for loop, the range object has full control on selecting the loop variable each time via the loop.

If you keep a close eye on older Python resources or even online Python example, you are likely to come across the xrange expression. Python version 2 has both the range and xrange. However, Python 3 doesn't have the xrange. The range expression of Python 3 is like the xrange expression in Python 2.

In Python 2, the range expression builds a data structure known as a list and this process can demand some time for a running program. In Python 2, the xrange expression eliminates the additional time. Hence, it is perfect for a big sequence. When creating loops using the for statement, developers of Python 2 prefer the xrange instead of the range to optimize the functionality of the code.

Chapter 10: Functions and Control Flow Statements in Python

This chapter is a comprehensive guide about functions. We will look at various components of function with examples. Let us go!

What is a Function?

Functions are organized and reusable code segments used to implement single or associated functionalities, which can improve the modularity of applications and the reuse rate of codes. Python provides many built-in functions, such as print (). Also, we can create our own functions, that is, custom functions.

Next, look at a code:

// display (" * ")

// display (" *** ")

// display ("*****")

If you need to output the above graphics in different parts of a program, it is not advisable to use the print () function to output each time. To improve writing efficiency and code reusability, we can organize code blocks with independent functions into a small module, which is called a function.

Defining Functions

We can define a function to achieve the desired functionality. Python definition functions begin with def, and the basic format for defining functions is as follows:

Def function {Enter the name here} (Enter parameters here):

"//Use this to define function String"

Function {Body}

Return expression

Note that if the parameter list contains more than one parameter, by default, the parameter values and parameter names match in the order defined in the function declaration.

Next, define a function that can complete printing information, as shown in Example below.

Example: Functions of Printing Information

defines a function that can print information.

def Overprint ():

print ('-----------------------------------')

print ('life is short, I use python')

print ('-----------------------------------')

Call Function

After defining a function, it is equivalent to having a piece of code with certain methods. To make these codes executable, you need to call it. Calling a function is very simple. You can call it by "function name ()".

For example, the code that calls the Useforprint function in the above section is as follows:

After the function is defined, the function will not be executed automatically and needs to be called

Useforprint ()

Parameters of Function

Before introducing the parameters of the function, let's first solve a problem. For example, it is required to define a function that is used to calculate the sum of two numbers and print out the calculated results. Convert the above requirements into codes.

The sample codes are as follows:

```
def thisisaddition ():

result = 62+12

print(result)
```

The functionality of the above function is to calculate the sum of 62 and 12. At this time, no matter how many times this function is called, the result will always be the same, and only the sum of two fixed numbers can be calculated, making this function very limited.

To make the defined function more general, that is, to calculate the sum of any two numbers, two parameters can be added when defining the function, and the two parameters can receive the value passed to the function.

Next, a case is used to demonstrate how a function passes parameters.

Example: Function Transfer Parameters

defines a function that receives 2 parameters

def thisisaddition (first, second):

third = first+second

print(third)

In Example, a function capable of receiving two parameters is defined. Where first is the first parameter for receiving the first value passed by the function; the second is the second parameter and receives the second value passed by the function. At this time, if you want to call the thisisaddition function, you need to pass two numeric values to the function's parameters.

The example code is as follows:

When calling a function with parameters, you need to pass data in parentheses.

thisisaddition (62, 12)

It should be noted that if a function defines multiple parameters, then when calling the function, the passed data should correspond to the defined parameters one by one.

Default Parameters

When defining a function, you can set a default value for its parameter, which is called the default parameter. When calling a function, because the default parameter has been assigned a value at the time of definition, it can be directly ignored, while other parameters must be passed in values. If the default parameter does not have an incoming value, the default value is directly used. If the default parameter passes in value, the new value passed in is used instead.

Next, we use a case to demonstrate the use of the default parameter.

Example: Default Parameters

```
def getdetails (input, time = 35):

# prints any incoming string

print ("Details:", input)

print ("Time:", time)

# calls printinfo function

printinfo (input="sydney")

printinfo (input="sydney", time=2232)
```

In an example, lines 1-4 define the getdetails function with two parameters. Among them, the input parameter has no default value, and age has already set the default value as the default parameter.

When calling the getdetails function, because only the value of the name parameter is passed in, the program uses the default value of the age parameter. When the getdetails function is called on line 7, the values of the name and age parameters are passed in at the same time so that the program will use the new value passed to the age parameter.

It should be noted that parameters with default values must be located at the back of the parameter list. Otherwise, the program will report an error, for example, add parameter sex to the getdetails function and place it at the back of the parameter list to look at the error information.

With this, we have completed a thorough explanation of functions in python. Control flow Statements

In this chapter, we will further continue discussing control statements briefly. A lot of examples are given to make you understand the essence of the topic. Let us dive into it.

What is the control flow statements?

All conditionals, loops and extra programming logic code that executes a logical structure are known as control flow statements. We already have an extensive introduction to conditionals and loops with various examples. Now, you should remember that the control flow statements we are going to learn now are very important for program execution. They can successfully skip or terminate or proceed with logic if used correctly. We will start learning about them now with examples. Let us go!

break statement

The break statement is used to end the entire loop (the current loop body) all at once. It is preceded by a logic.

for example, the following is a normal loop:

for sample in range (10):

```
print ("-------")
```

print sample

After the above loop statement is executed, the program will output integers from 0 to 9 in sequence. The program will not stop running until the loop ends. At this time, if you want the program to output only numbers from 0 to 2, you need to end the loop at the specified time (after executing the third loop statement).

Next, demonstrate the process of ending the loop with a break.

Example: break Statement

```
end=1
for end in range (10):
end+=1
print ("-------")
if end==3:
break
print(end)
```

In Example, when the program goes to the third cycle because the value of the end is 3, the program will stop and print the loop until then.

continue statement

The function of continue is to end this cycle and then execute the next cycle. It will look at the logical values and continue with the process.

Next, a case is used to demonstrate the use of the continue statement below.

Example continue statement

sample=1

for sample in range (10):

sample+=1

print ("-------")

if sample==3:

continue

print(sample)

In Example, when the program executes the third cycle because the value of sample is 3, the program will terminate this cycle without outputting the value of sample and immediately execute the next cycle.

Note:

(1) break/continue can only be used in a cycle, otherwise, it cannot be used alone.

(2) break/continue only works on the nearest loop in nested loops.

pass statement

Pass in Python is an empty statement, which appears to maintain the integrity of the program structure. Pass does nothing and is generally used as a placeholder.

The pass statement is used as shown in Example below.

Example pass Statement

for alphabet in 'University':

if letter == 'v':

pass

print ('This is the statement')

print ('Use this alphabet', letter)

print ("You can never see me again")

In Example above, when the program executes pass statements because pass is an empty statement, the program will ignore the statement and execute the statements in sequence.

else statement

Earlier, when learning if statements, else statements were found outside the scope of the if conditional syntax. In fact, in addition to judgment statements, while and for loops in Python can also use else statements. When used in a loop, the else statement is executed only after the loop is completed, that is, the break statement also skips the else statement block.

Next, we will demonstrate it through a case for your better understanding of the else block.

Example: else statement

result = 0

while result < 5:

 print (result, " is less than 5")

 result = result + 1

else:

```
print (result, " is not less than 5")
```

In Example, the else statement is executed after the while loop is terminated, that is, when the value of the result is equal to 5, the program executes the else statement.

With this, we have completed a short introduction to control flow statements in Python programming. It is always important to use control flow statements only when they are necessary. 📦 If they are used without any use case, they may start creating unnecessary blockages while programming. Let us go!

Conclusion:

For every programmer, the beginning is always the biggest hurdle. Once you set your mind to things and start creating a program, things automatically start aligning. The needless information is automatically omitted by your brain through its cognitive powers and understanding of the subject matter. All that remains then is a grey area that we discover further through various trials and errors.

There is no shortcut to learn to program in a way that will let you type codes 100% correctly, without a hint of an error, at any given time. Errors and exceptions appear even for the best programmers on earth. There is no programmer that I know of personally who can write programs without running into errors. These errors may be as simple as forgetting to close quotation marks, misplacing a comma, passing the wrong value, and so on. Expect yourself to be accompanied by these errors and try to learn how to avoid them in the long run. It takes practice, but there is a good chance you will end up being a programmer who runs into these issues only rarely.

We were excited when we began this workbook. Then came some arduously long tasks which quickly turned into irritating little chores that nagged us as programmers and made us think more than we normally would. There were times where some of us even felt like dropping the whole idea of being a programmer in the first place. But, every one of us who made it to this page, made it through with success.

Speaking of success, always know that your true success is never measured properly nor realized until you have hit a few failures along the road. It is a natural way of learning things. Every programmer, expert, or beginner, is bound to make mistakes. The difference between a good programmer and a bad one is that the former would learn and develop the skills while the latter would just resort to Google and locate an answer.

If you have chosen to be a successful Python programmer, know that there will be some extremely trying times ahead. The life of a programmer is rarely socially active, either unless your friend circle is made up of programmers only. You will struggle to manage your time at the start, but once you get the hang of things, you will start to perform exceptionally well. Everything will then start aligning, and you will begin to lead a more relaxed lifestyle as a programmer and as a human being.

Until that time comes, keep your spirits high and always be ready to encounter failures and mistakes. There is nothing to be ashamed of when going through such things. Instead, look back at your mistakes and learn from them to ensure they are not repeated in the future. You might be able to make programs even better or update the ones which are already functioning well enough.

Lastly, let me say it has been a pleasure to guide you through both these books and to be able to see you convert from a person who had no idea about Python to a programmer who now can code, understand and execute matters at will. Congratulations are in order. Here are digital cheers for you!

Print ("Bravo, my friend!")

I wish you the best of luck for your future and hope that one day, you will look back on this book and this experience as a life-changing event that led to a superior success for you as a professional programmer. Do keep an eye out for updates and ensure you visit the forums and other Python communities to gain the finest learning experience and knowledge to serve you even better when stepping into the more advanced parts of Python.

PYTHON FOR DATA SCIENCE:

The latest guide for the novice data scientist. Learn the principles of Python language to analyze and manage data. Machine learning and Scikit-learn sections included.

William Dimick

Introduction:

In this book we will lay down the foundational concepts of data science, starting with the term 'big data.' As we move along, we will steer the focus of our discussion towards the recognition of what exactly is data science and the various types of data we normally deal with within this field. By doing so, the readers will be able to gather a much-needed insight on the processes surrounding the niche of data science and, consequently, easily understand the concepts we put forward in this regarding the fields of data science and big data. After the theoretical explanatory sections, the book will conclude on working out some basic and common examples of Hadoop.

When handling data, the most common, traditional, and widely used management technique is the 'Relational Database Management Systems,' also known as 'RDBMS.' This technique applies to almost every dataset as it easily meets the dataset's required demands of processing; however, this is not the case for 'Big Data.' Before we can understand why such management techniques fail to process big data, we need first to understand what does the term 'Big Data' refers to. The name itself gives away a lot of the information regarding the data natures. Nevertheless, big data is a term that is used to define a collection of datasets that are very large and complex in size alone. Such datasets become difficult to process using traditional data management techniques and, thus, demand a new approach for handling them, as it is evident from the fact that the commonly used technique RDBMS has zero working compatibility with big data.

The core of data science is to employ methods and techniques that are the most suitable for the analysis of the sample dataset so that we can take out the essential bits of information contained in it. In other words, big data is like a raw mineral ore containing a variety of useful materials. Still, in its current form, its contents are unusable and no use to us. Data science is the refinery which essentially uses effective techniques to analyze this ore and then employ corresponding methods to extract its contents for us to use.

The world of big data is exponentially vast, and the use of data science with big data can be seen in almost every sector of the modern age, be it commercial, non-commercial, business, or even industrial settings. For instance, in a commercial setting, the corresponding companies use the data science and big data elements to chiefly get a better insight into the demands of their customers and information regarding the efficiency of their products, staff, manufacturing processes, etc. Consider Google's advertising department AdSense; it employs data science to analyze the big data (which is a collection of user internet data) to extract information to ensure that the person browsing the internet is seeing relevant advertisements. The uses of data science extend far and beyond what we can imagine. It is not possible to list all of its advantageous uses currently being employed in the modern-day. However, what we do know is that the majority of the datasets gathered by big companies all around the world are none other than big data. Data science is essential for these companies to analyze this data and benefit from the information it contains. Not only that, big educational institutions like Universities and research work also benefits from data science.

While venturing across the field of data science, you will soon come to realize that there is not one defined type of data. Instead, there are multiple categories under which data is classified, and each category of data requires an entirely different toolset to be processed.

Following are the seven major categories of data:

1. Structured Data

2. Unstructured Data

3. Natural Language Data

4. Machine Generated Data

5. Graph-based Data

6. Audio, Video, and Image Data
7. Streaming Data

As the name suggests, a collection of data that is organized according to a defined model and restricted in the record's corresponding data fields is known as structured data. For instance, data that is organized in the form of a table is known as structured data (such as Excel tables or in databases). To manage and analyze such data, a preferable method is to use the Structured Query Language or SQL. However, not all structured datasets are easily manageable; for instance, the family data tree is also a structured dataset, but it becomes difficult to process and analyze such structured datasets. In other words, there are some exceptions in these data categories that may demand another data processing technique.

Raw data is never structured; it is brought into a defined setting by the users. Hence, if we are given a data sample that is structured, then all is good, however, if the data is unstructured, then we must bring into a structured format before applying the SQL technique. Below is an example showing a dataset structured into an Excel table:

	Indicator ID	Dimension List	Timeframe	Numeric Value	Missing Value Flag	Confidence Inte
1	Indicator ID	Dimension List	Timeframe	Numeric Value	Missing Value Flag	Confidence Inte
2	214390830	Total (Age-adjusted)	2008	74.6%		73.8%
3	214390833	Aged 18-44 years	2008	59.4%		58.0%
4	214390831	Aged 18-24 years	2008	37.4%		34.6%
5	214390832	Aged 25-44 years	2008	66.9%		65.5%
6	214390836	Aged 45-64 years	2008	88.6%		87.7%
7	214390834	Aged 45-54 years	2008	86.3%		85.1%
8	214390835	Aged 55-64 years	2008	91.5%		90.4%
9	214390840	Aged 65 years and over	2008	94.6%		93.8%
10	214390837	Aged 65-74 years	2008	93.6%		92.4%
11	214390838	Aged 75-84 years	2008	95.6%		94.4%
12	214390839	Aged 85 years and over	2008	96.0%		94.0%
13	214390841	Male (Age-adjusted)	2008	72.2%		71.1%
14	214390842	Female (Age-adjusted)	2008	76.8%		75.9%
15	214390843	White only (Age-adjusted)	2008	73.8%		72.9%
16	214390844	Black or African American only (Age-adjusted)	2008	77.0%		75.0%
17	214390845	American Indian or Alaska Native only (Age-adjusted)	2008	66.5%		57.1%
18	214390846	Asian only (Age-adjusted)	2008	80.5%		77.7%
19	214390847	Native Hawaiian or Other Pacific Islander only (Age-adjusted)	2008	DSU		
20	214390848	2 or more races (Age-adjusted)	2008	75.6%		69.6%

Data usually found in emails is a common example of unstructured data. Hence to process and analyze the data, we must first filter it and bring it into a structured form.

One may argue that data contained in an email is also structured to some extent because there are fields such as the sender, the receiver, the subject. However, the reason why traditional structural data analyzing techniques do not apply to emails is that the data contained within them are either highly varying or context-specific. Moreover, the choice of words, the language used, and the intonations to refer to something in an email also varies, making the task even more complicated.

This is also a type of unstructured data, and it is also very complicated to process as we would need to factor in linguistics. Hence, for such datasets, the user must have a good understanding of various data science techniques in addition to linguistics. The main concern of the community

155

working with natural language processing is the lack of generalization in their models. Each model is trained specifically to one aspect, such as entity recognition, topic recognition, and summarization, etc. but these models fail to generalize over to other domains such as text completion and sentiment analysis. The reason is that language is ambiguous, and it is impossible to program and train machines to overcome this ambiguity when humans themselves have failed to do so.

As the name suggests, the data produced by a computer or its corresponding processes and applications without any external fiddling of humans is known as machine-generated data. Such types of data have become a major data resource as it is automated. To analyze and extract the information being contained within this machine-generated data, we would need to use very scalable tools. This is accordingly with this type of dataset that is not only high in volume but also in the speed generated. Data such as crash logs, web server logs, network logs, and even call record logs are all in nature, machine-generated data as shown in the example below:

```
CSIPERF:TXCOMMIT;313236
2014-11-28 11:36:13, Info        CSI    00000153 Creating NT transaction (seq
69), objectname [6]"(null)"
2014-11-28 11:36:13, Info        CSI    00000154 Created NT transaction (seq 69)
result 0x00000000, handle @0x4e54
2014-11-28 11:36:13, Info        CSI    00000155@2014/11/28:10:36:13.471
Beginning NT transaction commit...
2014-11-28 11:36:13, Info        CSI    00000156@2014/11/28:10:36:13.705 CSI perf
trace:
CSIPERF:TXCOMMIT;273983
2014-11-28 11:36:13, Info        CSI    00000157 Creating NT transaction (seq
70), objectname [6]"(null)"
2014-11-28 11:36:13, Info        CSI    00000158 Created NT transaction (seq 70)
result 0x00000000, handle @0x4e5c
2014-11-28 11:36:13, Info        CSI    00000159@2014/11/28:10:36:13.764
Beginning NT transaction commit...
2014-11-28 11:36:14, Info        CSI    0000015a@2014/11/28:10:36:14.094 CSI perf
trace:
CSIPERF:TXCOMMIT;386259
2014-11-28 11:36:14, Info        CSI    0000015b Creating NT transaction (seq
71), objectname [6]"(null)"
2014-11-28 11:36:14, Info        CSI    0000015c Created NT transaction (seq 71)
result 0x00000000, handle @0x4e5c
2014-11-28 11:36:14, Info        CSI    0000015d@2014/11/28:10:36:14.106
Beginning NT transaction commit...
2014-11-28 11:36:14, Info        CSI    0000015e@2014/11/28:10:36:14.428 CSI perf
trace:
CSIPERF:TXCOMMIT;375581
```

We must not confuse the terms 'graph' and 'graph theory.' The first one represents the geometrical representation of data in a graph, and any data can be made into a graph, but that does not necessarily change the nature of the data. The latter refers to the mathematical structure, which essentially is a model that connects the objects into a pair based on their inherent relationship with each other. Hence, we can also term such categories of data as Network data. This type of data emphasizes elements such as the adjacency and relationship of objects and the common structures found in graphs found in graph-based data are:

- Nodes

- Edges

- Properties

Graph-based data is most commonly seen on social media websites. Here's an example of a graph-based data representing many friends on a social network.

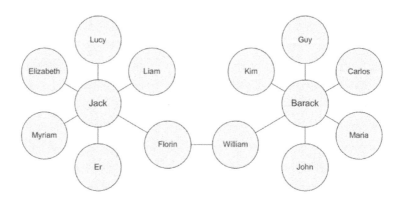

To query graph-based data, we normally use specialized query languages such as SPARQL.

Everyone is familiar with audio, image, and video data to a certain extent. However, out of all the data categories, audio, image, and video data are very difficult to deal with for a data scientist. This is partly because though we analyze this data, the computer must recognize elements, such as in image data, discerning between objects, and identifying them is a very difficult task. However, it is easy for the user. To deal with such categories of data, we usually implement deep learning models.

This category of data can take on the nature of any of the data categories mentioned previously. However, the aspect which makes it different from the other data categories is that in streaming data, the data only comes into the system after an event happens in real-time, unlike other categories where the data is loaded into the systems in the form of batches. The reason as to why streaming data is defined as an entirely different category is because we need an altogether different process to analyze and extract information from streaming data.

Chapter 1: What is Data Analysis?

Now that we have been able to spend some time taking a look at the ideas of python and what we can do with that coding language, it is time for us to move on to some of the things that we can do with all of that knowledge and all of the codes that we are looking. We are going to take a look here to see more about data analysis, and how we can use this to help us see some good results with our information as well.

Companies have spent a lot of time taking a look at data analysis and what it has been able to do for them. Data are all around us, and it seems like each day, tons of new information is available for us to work with regularly. Whether you are a business trying to learn more about your industry and your customers, or just an individual who has a question about a certain topic, you will be able to find a wealth of information to help you get started.

Many companies have gotten into a habit of gathering up data and learning how to make them work for their needs. They have found that there are a lot of insights and predictions inside these data to make sure that it is going to help them out in the future. If the data are used properly, and we can gain a good handle of those data, they can be used to help our business become more successful.

Once you have gathered the data, there is going to be some work to do. Just because you can gather up all of that data doesn't mean that you will be able to see what patterns are inside. This is where the process of data analysis is going to come into play to help us see some results as well. This is a process that is meant to ensure that we fully understand what is inside of our data and can make it easier to use all of that raw data to make some informed and smart business decisions.

To make this a bit further, data analysis is going to be a practice where we can take some of the raw data that our business has been collecting, and then organize and order it to ensure that it can be useful. During this process, the information that is the most useful is extracted and then used from that raw data.

The one thing that we need to be careful about when we are working with data analysis, though, is to be careful about the way that we manipulate the data that we have. It is really easy for us to go through and manipulate the data in the wrong way during the analysis phase, and then end up pushing certain conclusions or agendas that are not there. This is why we need to pay some close attention to when the data analysis is presented to us and to think critically about the data and the conclusions that we were able to get out of it.

If you are worried about a source that is being done, and if you are not sure that you can complete this kind of analysis without some biases in it, then it is important to find someone else to work on it or choose a different source. There is a lot of data out there, and it can help your business to see some results, but you have to be careful about these biases, or they will lead us to the wrong decisions in the end if we are not careful.

Besides, you will find that during the data analysis, the raw data that you will work with can take on a variety of forms. This can include things like observations, survey responses, and measurements, to name a few. The sources that you use for this kind of raw data will vary based on what you are hoping to get out of it, what your main question is all about, and more.

In its raw form, the data that we are gathering is going to be very useful to work with, but you may find that it is a bit overwhelming to work with as well. This is a problem that a lot of companies are going to have when they work with data analysis and something that you will have to spend some time exploring and learning more about, as well.

Over the time that you spend on data analysis and all of the steps that come with the process, the raw data are going to be ordered in a manner that makes it as useful to you as possible. For example, we may send out a survey and then will tally up the results that we get. This is going to be done because it helps us to see at a glance how many people decided to answer the survey at all, and how people were willing to respond to some of the specific questions that were on that survey.

In the process of going through and organizing the data, a trend is likely going to emerge, and sometimes more than one trend. And we are going to be then able to take some time to highlight these trends, usually in the write-up that is being done on the data. This needs to be highlighted because it ensures that the person who is reading that information is going to take note.

There are a lot of places that we are going to see this. For example, in a casual kind of survey that we may try to do, you may want to figure out the preferences between men and women of what ice cream flavors they like the most. In this survey, maybe we find out that women and men are going to express a fondness for chocolate. Depending on who is using this information and what they are hoping to get out of that information, it could be something that the researcher is going to find very interesting.

Modeling the data that is found out of the survey, or out of another form of data analysis, with the use of mathematics and some of the other tools out there, can sometimes exaggerate the points of interest, such as the ice cream preferences from before, in our data, which is going to make it so much easier for anyone who is looking over the data, especially the researcher, to see what is going on there.

In addition to taking a look at all of the data that you have collected and sorted through, you will need to do a few other parts as well. These are all meant to help the person who needs this information to read through it and see what is inside and what they can do with all of that data. It is the way that they can use the information to see what is going on, the complex relationships that are there, and so much more.

This means that we need to spend our time with some write-ups of the data, graphs, charts, and other ways to represent and show the data to those who need it the most. This will form one of the final steps that come with data analysis. These methods are designed in a manner to distill and refine the data so that the readers are then able to glean some of the interesting information from it, without having to go back through the raw data and figure out what is there all on their own.

Summarizing the data in these steps is going to be critical, and it needs to be done in a good and steady manner as well. Doing this is going to be critical to helping to support some of the arguments that are made with that data, as is presenting the data clearly and understandably. During this phase, we have to remember that it is not always possible that the person who needs that summary and who will use it to make some important decisions for the business will be data scientists. They need it all written out in a simple and easy to understand this information. This is why the data has to be written out in a manner that is easy to understand and read through.

Often this is going to be done with some sort of data visualization. There are many choices of visuals that we can work with, and working with some kind of graph or chart is a good option as well. Working with the method that is the best for your needs and the data that we are working with is going to be the best way to determine the visual that is going to be the best for you.

Many times, reading through information that is in a more graphical format is going to be easier to work with than just reading through the data and hoping it to work the best way possible. You could just have it all in a written form if you would like, but this is not going to be as easy to read through nor as efficient. To see some of those complex relationships quickly and efficiently, working with a visual is going to be one of the best options to choose from.

Even though we need to spend some time working with a visual of the data to make it easier to work with and understand, it is fine to add in some of the raw data as the appendix, rather than just throwing it out. This allows the person who is going to work with that data regularly a chance to check your resources and your specific numbers and can help to bolster some of the results that you are getting overall.

If you are the one who is getting the results of the data analysis, make sure that when you get the conclusions and the summarized data from your data scientist that you go through and view them more critically. You should take the time to ask where the data comes from is going to be important, and you should also take some time to ask about the method of sampling that was used for all of this as well when the data was collected. Knowing the size of the sample is important as well.

Chapter 2: The Basics of the Python Language

Python language is one of the best coding languages that you can start handling for your first data science project. This is a fantastic language that capable to take on all of the work that you want to do with data science and has the power that is needed to help create some great machine learning algorithms. With that said, it is still a great option for beginners because it has been designed to work with those who have never done programming before. While you can choose to work with the R programming language as well, you will find that the Python language is one of the best options because of its ease of use and power that combines.

Before we dive into how Python can work with some of the things that you would like to do with data science, we first need to take some time to look at the basics of the Python language. Python is a great language to look through, and you will be able to learn how to do some of the codings that you need to in no time. Some of the different types of coding that you can do with the Python language will include:

The Statements

The first thing that we are going to take a moment to look through when it comes to our Python language is the keywords. This is going to focus on the lines or sentences that you would like to have the compiler show up on your screen. You will need to use some of the keywords that we will talk about soon, and then you can tell the compiler what statements to put up on the screen. If you would like to leave a message on the screen such as what we can do with the Hello, World! The program, you will need to use that as your statement, and the print keyword, so the compiler knows how to behave.

The Python Operators

We can also take some time to look at what is known as the Python operators. These are often going to get ignored when it comes time to write out codes because they don't seem like they are that important. But if you skip out on writing them, they are going to make it so that your code will not work the way that you would like. We can focus on several different types of Python operators, so making sure that you know what each kind is all about, and when to add these into your code will make a world of difference as well.

The Keywords

The keywords are another important part of our Python code that we need to take a look at. These are going to be the words that we need to reserve because they are responsible for giving the compiler the instructions or the commands that you would like for it to use. These key words ensure that the code is going to perform the way that you would like it for the whole time.

These keywords need to be reserved, so make sure that you are not using them in the wrong places. If you do not use these keywords in the right manner, or you don't put them in the right place, then the compiler is going to end up with some issues understanding what you would like it to do, and you will not be able to get the results that you want. Make sure to learn the important keywords that come with the Python language and learn how to put them in the right spot of your code to get the best results with it.

Working with Comments

As we work with the Python coding, there are going to be times when we need to spend our time working with something that is known as a comment. This is going to be one of the best things that we can do to make sure that we can name a part of the code, or when we want to leave a little note for yourself or another programmer, then you are going to need to work with some of the comments as well.

These comments are going to be a great option to work with. They are going to allow you to leave a nice message in the code, and the compiler will know that it should just skip over that part of the code, and not read through it at all. It is as simple as that and can save you a lot of hassle and work inside of any code you are doing.

So, any time that you would like to write out a comment inside of your Python code, you just need to use the # symbol, and then the compiler will know that it is supposed to skip over that part of the code and not read it. We can add in as many of these comments as we would like into the code. Just remember to keep these to the number that is necessary, rather than going overboard with this, because it ensures that we are going to keep the code looking as nice and clean as possible.

The Python Class

One thing that is extremely important when it comes to working with Python, and other similar languages, is the idea that the language is separated into classes and objects. The objects are meant to fit into the classes that you create, giving them more organization, and ensuring that the different parts are going to fit together the way that you would like without trouble. In some of the older types of programming languages, the organization was not there, and this caused a lot of confusion and frustration for those who were just starting.

These classes are simply going to be a type of container that can hold onto your objects, the ones that you write out, and are based on actual items in the real world and other parts of the code. You will need to make sure that you name these classes in the right manner, and then have them listed out in the code in the right spot to make sure they work and call up the objects that you need. And placing the right kinds of objects into the right class is going to be important as well.

You can store anything that you want inside a class that you design, but you must ensure that things that are similar end up in the same class. The items don't have to be identical to each other, but when someone takes a look at the class that you worked on, they need to be able to see that those objects belong together and make sense to be together.

For example, you don't have just to put cars into the same class, but you could have different vehicles in the same class. You could have items that are considered food. You can even have items that are all the same color. You get some freedom when creating the classes and storing objects in those classes, but when another programmer looks at the code, they should be able to figure out what the objects inside that class are about and those objects should share something in common.

Classes are very important when it comes to writing out your code. These are going to hold onto the various objects that you write in the code and can ensure that everything is stored properly. They will also make it easier for you to call out the different parts of your code when you need them for execution.

How to Name Your Identifiers

Inside the Python language, there are going to be several identifiers that we need to spend some time on. Each of these identifiers is going to be important, and they are going to make a big difference in some of the different parts of the code that you can work with. They are going to come to us under a lot of different names, but you will find that they are going to follow the same kinds of rules when it comes to naming them, and that can make it a lot easier for a beginner to work with as well.

To start with, you can use a lot of different types of characters in order to handle the naming of the identifiers that you would like to work with. You can use any letter of the alphabet that you would like, including uppercase and lowercase, and any combination of the two that you would like. Using numbers and the underscore symbol is just fine in this process as well.

With this in mind, there are going to be a few rules that you have to remember when it comes to naming your identifiers. For example, you are not able to start a name with the underscore symbol or with a number. So, writing something like 3puppies or _threepuppies would not work. But you can do it with something like threepuppies for the name. A programmer also won't be able to add in spaces between the names either. You can write out threepuppies or three_puppies if you would like, but do not add the space between the two of them.

In addition to some of these rules, we need to spend some time looking at one other rule that is important to remember. Pick out a name for your identifier that is easy to remember and makes sense for that part of the code. This is going to ensure that you can understand the name and that you will be able to remember it later on when you need to call it up again.

Python Functions

Another topic that we are going to take a quick look at here as we work with the Python language is the idea of the Python functions. These are going to be a set of expressions that can also be statements inside of your code as well. You can have the choice to give them a name or let them remain anonymous. They are often the first-class objects that we can explore as well, meaning that your restrictions on how to work with them will be lower than we will find with other class objects.

Now, these functions are very diversified and there are many attributes that you can use when you try to create and bring up those functions. Some of the choices that you have with these functions include:

- __doc__: This is going to return the docstring of the function that you are requesting.
- Func_default: This one is going to return a tuple of the values of your default argument.
- Func_globals: This one will return a reference that points to the dictionary holding the global variables for that function.
- Func_dict: This one is responsible for returning the namespace that will support the attributes for all your arbitrary functions.
- Func_closure: This will return to you a tuple of all the cells that hold the bindings for the free variables inside of the function.

Chapter 3: Using Pandas

It would be difficult to delve deeper into the technical aspect of data science and analysis without a refresher course on the basics of data analysis. Come to think of it, data science, new as it is, is still a generally broad topic of study. Many books have tried to specifically define what data science and being a data scientist means. After all, it was voted one of the most highly coveted jobs this decade, according to surveys done by Google. Unfortunately, the sheer wide and general variety of data science topics ranging from Artificial Intelligence to Machine Learning means that it is difficult to place data science under one large umbrella. Despite the attempt to define data science, having to clearly define it is a daunting task and one that shouldn't be taken lightly.

However, one fact remains about data science that could be consistently said throughout the various practices of data science: the use of software and programming basics is just as integral as the analysis of the data. Having the ability to use and create models and artificially intelligent programs is integral to the success of having clean, understandable, and readable data. The discussions you will find in this book will regard the latest and more advanced topics of interest in the topic of data science, as well as a refresher course on the basics.

Pandas

The core of Data Science lies in Python. Python is one of the easiest and most intuitive languages out there. For more than a decade, Python has absolutely dominated the market when it comes to programming. Python is one of the most flexible programming languages to date. It is extremely common, and honestly, it is also one of the more readable languages. As one of the more popular languages right now, Python is complete with an ever-supporting community and deep and extensive support modules. If you were to open GitHub right now, you'd find thousands of repositories filled with millions of lines of Python code. As flexible programming, python is used for machine learning, deep learning applications, 2D imagery, and 3D animation.

If you have no experience in Python, then it is best to learn it before progressing through further sections of this book.

Assuming that you do have a basic understanding of Python and that coding in this language has almost become natural to you, the following sections will make more sense. If you have experience in Python, you should at least have heard about Pandas and Scikit Library.

Essentially, Pandas is a data analysis tool used to manipulate and analyze data. It is particularly useful as it offers methods to build and create data structures as well as methods used to manipulate numerical tables and time series. As an open-source library, the Pandas library is built on top of NumPy, indicating that Pandas requires the prior installation of NumPy to operate.

Pandas make use of data frames, which is essentially a two-dimensional array with labeled axes. It is often used as it provides methods to handle missing data easily, efficient methods to slice, reshape, merge, and concatenate data as well as providing us with powerful time series tools to work with. Learning to write in Pandas and NumPy is essential in the beginning steps of becoming a Data Scientist.

A Pandas array looks like the sample photo below:

	Item	Price
0	A	2
1	B	3

Now, the data frame doesn't look too difficult to understand, does it? It's similar to the product lists you see when you check out the grocery.

This tiny 2x2 data frame is a perfect encapsulation of one of the things that this has been trying to show. Data Science isn't as tricky, nor is it as difficult as some people make it seem because Data Science is simply the process of making sense of data tables given to you. This process of analyzing and making sense is something that we've been unconsciously practicing for our whole lives, from us trying to make sense of our personal finance to us looking at data tables of products that we're trying to sell.

Let's dive in further as to how to use this powerful library. As it is one of the most popular tools for data manipulation and analysis, Pandas data structures were designed to make data analysis in the real-world significantly easier. There are many ways to use Pandas, and often, the choices in the functionality of the program may be overwhelming. In this section, we'll begin to shed some light on the subject matter and, hopefully, begin to learn some Pandas functionality.

Pandas have two primary components that you will be manipulating and seeing a lot of; these are the Series and the DataFrame. There is not much difference between these two, besides a series essentially being the representative of a smaller DataFrame. A series is simply one column of data. At the same time, a DataFrame is a multi-dimensional table, meaning that it has multiple combinations of columns and arrows that are made up of a collection of

Series. We can create these DataFrames through many options, such as lists or tuples, but for this tutorial, we'll just be using a simple dictionary.

Let's create a dictionary that symbolizes the fruit that a customer bought, and as a value connected to the fruit, the amount that each customer purchases.

```
data= {

    'apples': [3,2,0,1],

    'oranges': [0,3,7,2]

}
```

Great! We now have our first DataFrame. However, this isn't accessible to Pandas yet. For Pandas to be able to access the DataFrame, we need to pass in the dictionary into the Pandas DataFrame constructor. We simply type in:

```
customer_purchases=pd. DataFrame(data)

print(purchases)
```

And it should output something like this:

```
    applesoranges

030

123

207
```

312

Basically, what happened here was that each (key, value) item in the dictionary "data" corresponds to a column in the data frame. Understanding the data that we placed, here it could be said that the first customer bought three apples and 0 oranges, the second customer bought two apples and three oranges, the third customer bought no apples and seven oranges, and so on. The column on the right refers to the index of the item in relation to its position on the sequence. In programming, counting an index doesn't begin with one, as the counting begins, instead, with 0. So, this means that the first item has an index of zero, the second has an index of one, the third has an index of two, and so and so forth. We can now call the items in a sequence based on their index. So, by calling 'apples [0]' where we use apples as our key and then 0 as our index, it should return the value of '3'.

However, we can also replace the value of our index. To do that, we input the following line of code.

purchases =pd. DataFrame (data, index= ['June', 'Robert,' 'Lily,' 'David'])

print(purchases)

Now, instead of using the index positions to locate the item in the sequence, we can use the customer's name to find the order. For this, we could use the *loc* function, which is written in this manner: "DataFrame.loc[x]" where DataFrame is the name of the dataset that you would like to access, and loc is the location of the item that you would like to access. Essentially, this function accesses a group of rows and columns through the index or index names. For example, we can now access June's orders through the command purchases.loc['June'], which can be found on index 0. This would return the following:

Apples   3

oranges   0

Name: June dtype: int64

We can learn more about locating, accessing and extracting DataFrames later, but for now, we should move on to loading files for you to use.

Honestly, the process of loading data into DataFrames is quite simple. Assuming you already have a DataFrame that you would like to use from an outside source, the process of creating a DataFrame out of it is much simpler than loading it into a google drive. However, we will still be using the purchases dataset as an example of a CSV file. CSV files are comma-separated value files that allow for data to be used and accessed in a tabular format. CSV files are basically spreadsheets but with an ending extension of .csv. These can also be accessed with almost any spreadsheet program, such as Microsoft Excel or Google Spreadsheets. In Pandas, we can access CSV files like this:

df=pd. read_csv('purchases.csv')

df

If you input it right, your text editor should output something similar to this:

	Unnamed:0	apples	ORANGES
0	June	3	0
1	Robert	2	3
2	Lily	0	7

3	David	1	
			2

What happened? Well, basically, it created another DataFrame, and it assumed that the newly renamed indexes of June, Robert, Lily, and David were already parts of the DataFrame. As a result, it ended up giving out new indexes to the DataFrame, adding a new column of 0 to 3. However, we can designate a certain column to be our index; in that case, we can input:

df=pd. read_csv ('purchases.csv', index_col=0)

df

The lines of code above will output that your names column will still remain to be the index column. Essentially, we're setting the index to be column zero. However, you will find that more often than not, CSV's won't add an index column to your DataFrame so you can forget about this step, and most probably, nothing will change.

After loading in your dataset, it is best to make sure that you loaded in the correct one - while also making sure that your index column is properly set. In that case, you could simply type in the name of the dataset you're using into

Jupyter notebooks, and it would show the whole dataset. It is always a good idea to eyeball the data you're using so that you can quickly fix mistakes and avoid any future problems down the road.

Aside from CSVs, we can also read JSON files, which are basically stored versions of dictionary files in Python. It is important to note that JSON allows indexes to work through a process called nesting, so that means that this time, our index should come back to us correctly. Accessing JSON files works essentially the same as accessing CSV files, we simply input the following lines of code.

df=pd. read_json ('purchases. json')

df

Notice that we are using the same dataset to load both the CSV and JSON files. Why does this work? Well, these two really only look at the extension of the files to make sure that they could load it. As long as it looks like something even remotely related to a DataFrame, your computer is smart enough to recognize the fact that it is a dataset and read it from there.

Furthermore, we can also read data from SQL databases. SQL stands for Structured Query Language and is the standard language for dealing with a concept known as Relational Databases. What can SQL do? It executes queries, retrieves data, insert, update, and delete records all from a database, as well as giving you the ability to create tables and entirely new databases from scratch.

Chapter 4: Working with Python for Data Science

Programming languages help us to expand our theoretical knowledge to something that can happen. Data science, which usually needs a lot of data to make things happen, will by nature take advantage of programming languages to make the data organize well for further steps of the model development. So, let us start learning about Python for a better understanding of the topic.

Why Python Is Important?

To illustrate this problem more vividly, we might as well assume that we have a small partner named Estella. She just got a job related to Data Science after graduating from the math department. On her first day at work, she was enthusiastic and eager to get in touch with this dude-new industry. But she soon found herself facing a huge difficulty:

The data needed to process the work is not stored in her personal computer, but in remote servers, some in traditional relational databases, and some in Hadoop clusters. Unlike Windows, which is mostly used by personal computers, Linux-like systems are used on remote servers. Estella is not used to this operating system because the familiar graphical interface is missing. All operations, such as the simplest reading of files, need to be programmed by oneself. Therefore, Estella is eager to find a programming language that is simple to write, easy to learn and easy to use.

What is more fatal is that the familiar data modeling software, such as SPSS and MATLAB, cannot be used in the new working environment. However, Estella often uses some basic algorithms provided by this software in her daily work, such as linear regression and logical regression. Therefore, she hopes that the programming language she finds will also have a library of algorithms that can be used easily, and of course, it is better to be free of charge.

The whole process is very similar to Estella's favorite table tennis. The assumption is sent to the data as a "ball", and then the adjustment is made according to the "return ball" of the data, and the above actions are repeated. Therefore, Estella added one more item to her request: the programming language can be modified and used at any time without compilation. It is better to have an immediate response command window so that she can quickly verify her ideas. After a search, Estella excitedly told everyone that she had found an IT tool that met all her requirements that is Python.

I hope you have got a good layman introduction on why programming language is important for Data Science. In the next sections, we will describe the language and its basic functions in detail.

What Is Python?

Python is an object-oriented and interpretive computer program language. Its syntax is simple and contains a set of standard libraries with complete functions, which can easily accomplish many common tasks. Speaking of Python, its birth is also quite interesting. During the Christmas holidays in 1989, Dutch programmer Guido van Rossum stayed at home and found himself doing nothing. So, to pass the "boring" time, he wrote the first version of Python.

Python is widely used. According to statistics from GitHub, an open-source community, it has been one of the most popular programming languages in the past 10 years and is more popular than traditional C, C++ languages, and C# which is very commonly used in Windows systems. After using Python for some time, Estella thinks it is a programming language specially designed for non-professional programmers.

Its grammatical structure is very concise, encouraging everyone to write as much code as possible that is easy to understand and write as little code as possible.

Functionally speaking, Python has a large number of standard libraries and third-party libraries. Estella develops her application based on these existing programs, which can get twice the result with half the effort and speed up the development progress.

Python's Position in Data Science

After mastering Python as a programming language, Estella can do many interesting things, such as writing a web crawler, collecting needed data from the Internet, developing a task scheduling system, updating the model regularly, etc.

Below we will describe how the Python is used by Estella for Data Science applications:

Data Cleaning

After obtaining the original data, Estella will first do preliminary processing on the data, such as unifying the case of the string, correcting the wrong data, etc. This is also the so-called "clean up" of "dirty" data to make the data more suitable for analysis. With Python and its third-party library pandas, Estella can easily complete this step of work.

Data Visualization

Estella uses Matplotlib to display data graphically. Before extracting the features, Estella can get the first intuitive feeling of the data from the graph and enlighten the thinking. When communicating with colleagues in other departments, information can be clearly and effectively conveyed and communicated with the help of graphics so that those insights can be put on paper.

Feature Extraction

In this step, Richard usually associates relevant data stored in different places, for example, integrating customer basic information and customer shopping information through customer ID. Then transform the data and extract the variables useful for modeling. These variables are called features. In this process, Estella will use Python's NumPy, SciPy, pandas, and PySpark.

Model Building

The open-source libraries sci-kit-learn, StatsModels, Spark ML, and TensorFlow cover almost all the commonly used basic algorithms. Based on these algorithm bases and according to the data characteristics and algorithm assumptions, Estella can easily build the basic algorithms together and create the model she wants.

The above four things are also the four core steps in Data Science. No wonder Estella, like most other data scientists, chose Python as a tool to complete his work.

Python Installation

After introducing so many advantages of Python, let's quickly install it and feel it for ourselves.

Python has two major versions: Python 2 and Python 3. Python 3 is a higher version with new features that Python 2 does not have. However, because Python 3 was not designed with backward compatibility in mind, Python 2 was still the main product in actual production (although Python 3 had been released for almost 10 years at the time of writing this book). Therefore, it is recommended that readers still use Python 2 when installing completely. The code accompanying this book is compatible with Python 2 and Python 3.

The following describes how to install Python and the libraries listed in section

It should be noted that the distributed Machine Learning library Spark ML involves the installation of Java and Scala, and will not be introduced here for the time being.

Installation Under Windows

The author does not recommend people to develop under Windows system. There are many reasons, the most important of which is that in the era of big data, as mentioned by Estella earlier, data is stored under the Linux system. Therefore, in production, the programs developed by data scientists will eventually run in the Linux environment. However, the compatibility between Windows and Linux is not good, which easily leads to the development and debugging of good programs under Windows, and cannot operate normally under the actual production environment.

If the computer the reader uses is a Windows system, he can choose to install a Linux virtual machine and then develop it on the virtual machine. If readers insist on using Windows, due to the limitation of TensorFlow under Windows, they can only choose to install Python 3. Therefore, the tutorial below this section is also different from other sections, using Python 3. Anaconda installed several applications under Windows, such as IPython, Jupyter, Conda, and Spyder. Below we will explain some of them in detail.

Conda

It is a management system for the Python development environment and open source libraries. If readers are familiar with Linux, Conda is equivalent to pip+virtualenv under Linux. Readers can list installed Python libraries by entering "Condolist" on the command line.

Spyder

It is an integrated development environment (IDE) specially designed for Python for scientific computing. If readers are familiar with the mathematical analysis software MATLAB, they can find that Spyder and MATLAB are very similar in syntax and interface.

Installation Under MAC

Like Anaconda's version of Windows, Anaconda's Mac version does not contain a deep learning library TensorFlow, which needs to be installed using pip (Python Package Management System). Although using pip requires a command line, it is very simple to operate and even easier than installing Anaconda. Moreover, pip is more widely used, so it is suggested that readers try to install the required libraries with pip from the beginning. The installation method without Anaconda is described below.

Starting with Mac OS X 10.2, Python is preinstalled on macs. For learning purposes, you can choose to use the pre-installed version of Python ; directly. If it is for development purposes, pre-installed Python is easy to encounter problems when installing third-party libraries, and the latest version of Python needs to be reinstalled. The reader is recommended to reinstall Python here.

Installation Under Linux

Similar to Mac, Anaconda also offers Linux versions. Please refer to the instructions under Windows and the accompanying code for specific installation steps.

There are many versions of Linux, but due to space limitations, the only installation on Ubuntu is described here. The following installation guide may also run on other versions of Linux, but we have only tested these installation steps on Ubuntu 14.04 or later.

Although Ubuntu has pre-installed Python, the version is older, and it is recommended to install a newer version of Python.

Install Python

install [insert command here]

Pip is a Python software package management system that facilitates us to install the required third-party libraries. The steps for installing pip are as follows.

1) Open the terminal

2) Enter and run the following code

Python shell

Python, as a dynamic language, is usually used in two ways: it can be used as a script interpreter to run edited program scripts; At the same time, Python provides a real-time interactive command window (Python shell) in which any Python statement can be entered and run. This makes it easy to learn, debug, and test Python statements.

Enter "Python" in the terminal (Linux or Mac) or command prompt (Windows) to start the Python shell.

1) You can assign values to variables in the Python shell and then calculate the variables used. And you can always use these variables as long as you don't close the shell. As shown in lines 1 to 3 of the code. It is worth noting that Python is a so-called dynamic type language, so there is no need to declare the type of a variable when assigning values to variables.

2) Any Python statement can be run in the Python shell, as shown in the code, so some people even use it as a calculator.

3) You can also import and use a third-party library in the shell, as shown. It should be noted that as shown in the code, the third-party library "numpy" can be given an alias, such as "np" while being imported. When "numpy" is needed

later, it is replaced by "np" to reduce the amount of character input.

Chapter 5: Indexing and Selecting Arrays

Array indexing is very much similar to List indexing with the same techniques of item selection and slicing (using square brackets). The methods are even more similar when the array is a vector.

Example:

In []: # Indexing a vector array (values)
 values
 values [0]   # grabbing 1st item
 values [-1] # grabbing last item
 values [1:3] # grabbing 2nd & 3rd item
 values [3:8] # item 4 to 8

Out []: array ([1.33534821, 1.73863505, 0.1982571, -0.47513784,   1.80118596, -1.73710743, -0.24994721, 1.41695744, -0.28384007, 0.58446065])

Out []: 1.3353482110285562

Out []: 0.5844606470172699

Out []: array ([1.73863505, 0.1982571])

Out []: array ([-0.47513784, 1.80118596, -1.73710743, - 0.24994721, 1.41695744])

The main difference between arrays and lists is in the broadcast property of arrays. When a slice of a list is assigned to another variable, any changes on that new variable does not affect the original list. This is seen in the example below:

```
In []: num_list = list (range (11)) # list from 0-10
num_list                # display list
list_slice = num_list [:4]   # first 4 items
list_slice                # display slice
list_slice [:] = [5,7,9,3]   # Re-assigning elements

list_slice                # display updated values
# checking for changes
print (' The list changed!') if list_slice == num_list [:4] \
else print (' no changes in original list')
```

Out []: [0, 1, 2, 3, 4, 5, 6, 7, 8, 9, 10]

Out []: [0, 1, 2, 3]

Out []: [5, 7, 9, 3]

no changes in the original list

For arrays, however, a change in the slice of an array also updates or broadcasts to the original array, thereby changing its values.

In []: # Checking the broadcast feature of arrays

num_array = np. arrange (11)   # *array from 0-10*

num_array   # *display array*

array_slice = num_array [:4] # *first 4 items*

array_slice   # *display slice*

array_slice [:] = [5,7,9,3]   # *Re-assigning elements*

array_slice   # *display updated values*
num_array

Out []: array ([0, 1, 2, 3, 4, 5, 6, 7, 8, 9, 10])

Out []: array ([0, 1, 2, 3])

Out []: array ([5, 7, 9, 3])

Out []: array ([5, 7, 9, 3, 4, 5, 6, 7, 8, 9, 10])

This happens because Python tries to save memory allocation by allowing slices of an array to be like shortcuts or links to the actual array. This way it doesn't have to allocate a separate memory location to it. This is especially ingenious in the case of large arrays whose slices can also take up significant memory. However, to take up a slice of an array without broadcast, you can create a 'slice of a copy' of the array. The array. copy () method is called to create a copy of the original array.

In []: # Here is an array allocation without broadcast
num_array   # Array from the last example

# copies the first 4 items of the array copy
array_slice = num_array. copy () [:4]
array_slice
 # display array
array_slice [:] = 10

 # re-assign array

array_slice

 # display updated values

num_array

 # checking original list

Out []: array ([5, 7, 9, 3, 4, 5, 6, 7, 8, 9, 10])

Out []: array ([5, 7, 9, 3])

Out []: array ([10, 10, 10, 10])

Out []: array ([5, 7, 9, 3, 4, 5, 6, 7, 8, 9, 10])

Notice that the original array remains unchanged.

For two-dimensional arrays or matrices, the same indexing and slicing methods work. However, it is always easy to consider the first dimension as the rows and the other as the columns. To select any item or slice of items, the index of the rows and columns are specified. Let us illustrate this with a few examples:

Example 63: Grabbing elements from a matrix

There are two methods for grabbing elements from a matrix: array_name[row][col] or array_name [row, col].

In []: # Creating the matrix
 matrix = np. array (([5,10,15], [20,25,30], [35,40,45]))

 matrix   #display matrix
 matrix [1]   # Grabbing second row
 matrix [2][0] # Grabbing 35

matrix [0:2] # Grabbing first 2 rows

matrix [2,2] # *Grabbing 45*

Out []: array ([[5, 10, 15],

[20, 25, 30],

[35, 40, 45]])

Out []: array ([20, 25, 30])

Out []: 35

Out []: array ([[5, 10, 15],
[20, 25, 30]])

Out []: 45

Tip: It is recommended to use the array_name [row, col] method, as it saves typing and is more compact. This will be the convention for the rest of this section.

To grab columns, we specify a slice of the row and column. Let us try to grab the second column in the matrix and assign it to a variable column_slice.

In []: # Grabbing the second column

column_slice = matrix [: 1:2] # *Assigning to variable*

column_slice

Out []: array ([[10],

    [25],

    [40]]])

Let us consider what happened here. To grab the column slice, we first specify the row before the comma. Since our column contains elements in all rows, we need all the rows to be included in our selection, hence the ':' sign for all. Alternatively, we could use '0:', which might be easier to understand. After selecting the row, we then choose the column by specifying a slice from '1:2', which tells Python to grab from the second item up to (but not including) the third item. Remember, Python indexing starts from zero.

Exercise: Try to create a larger array, and use these indexing techniques to grab certain elements from the array. For example, here is a larger array:

In []: # 5 × 10 Array of even numbers between 0 and 100.
large_array = np. arrange (0,100,2). reshape (5,10)
large_array   # show

Out []: array ([[0, 2, 4, 6, 8, 10, 12, 14, 16, 18],

    [20, 22, 24, 26, 28, 30, 32, 34, 36, 38],

    [40, 42, 44, 46, 48, 50, 52, 54, 56, 58],

[60, 62, 64, 66, 68, 70, 72, 74, 76, 78],
[80, 82, 84, 86, 88, 90, 92, 94, 96, 98]])

Tip: Try grabbing single elements and rows from random arrays you create. After getting very familiar with this, try selecting columns. The point is to try as many combinations as possible to get you familiar with the approach. If the slicing and indexing notations are confusing, try to revisit the section under list or string slicing and indexing.

Click this link to revisit the examples on slicing: List indexing

Conditional selection

Consider a case where we need to extract certain values from an array that meets a Boolean criterion. NumPy offers a convenient way of doing this without having to use loops.

Example: Using conditional selection

Consider this array of odd numbers between 0 and 20. Assuming we need to grab elements above 11. We first have to create the conditional array that selects this:

In []: odd_array = np. arrange (1,20,2)   *# Vector of odd numbers*

odd_array   *# Show vector*
bool_array = odd_array > 11   *# Boolean conditional array*

bool_array

Out []: array ([1, 3, 5, 7, 9, 11, 13, 15, 17, 19])

Out []: array ([False, False, False, False, False, False, True,
    True, True, True])

Notice how the bool_array evaluates to True at all instances
where the elements of the odd_array meet the Boolean
criterion.

The Boolean array itself is not usually so useful. To return
the values that we need, we will pass the Boolean_array
into the original array to get our results.

In []: useful_Array = odd_array[bool_array] # *The values
    we want*

useful_Array

Out []: array ([13, 15, 17, 19])

Now, that is how to grab elements using conditional
selection. There is however a more compact way of doing
this. It is the same idea, but it reduces typing.

Instead of first declaring a Boolean_array to hold our true
values, we just pass the condition into the array itself, as we
did for useful_array.

In []: # This code is more compact
compact = odd_array[odd_array>11] # *One line*
compact

Out []: array ([13, 15, 17, 19])

See how we achieved the same result with just two lines? It is recommended to use this second method, as it saves coding time and resources. The first method helps explain how it all works. However, we would be using the second method for all other instances in this book.

Exercise: The conditional selection works on all arrays (vectors and matrices alike). Create a two 3 $\times$ 3 array of elements greater than 80 from the 'large_array' given in the last exercise.

Hint: use the reshape method to convert the resulting array into a 3 $\times$ 3 matrix.

NumPy Array Operations

Finally, we will be exploring basic arithmetical operations with NumPy arrays. These operations are not unlike that of integer or float Python lists.

Array – Array Operations

In NumPy, arrays can operate with and on each other using various arithmetic operators. Things like the addition of two arrays, division, etc.

Example 65:

In []: # Array - Array Operations

# Declaring two arrays of 10 elements
Array1 = np. arrange (10). reshape (2,5)
Array2 = np. random. rind (10). reshape (2,5)
Array1; Array2   # Show the arrays

# Addition
Array_sum = Array1 + Array2
Array_sum   # show result array

#Subtraction
Array_minus = Array1 - Array2
Array_minus   # Show array

# Multiplication
Array_product = Array1 * Array2
Array_product   # Show

# Division
Array_divide = Array1 / Array2
Array_divide   # Show

Out []: array ([[0, 1, 2, 3, 4],
    [5, 6, 7, 8, 9]])

array ([[2.09122638, 0.45323217, -0.50086442,
1.00633093, 1.24838264], [1.64954711, -
0.93396737, 1.05965475, 0.78422255, -
1.84595505]])

array ([[2.09122638, 1.45323217, 1.49913558, 4.00633093,
5.24838264], [6.64954711, 5.06603263, 8.05965475,
8.78422255, 7.15404495]])

array ([[-2.09122638,
0.54676783, 2.50086442, 1.99366907, 2.75161736],
[3.35045289, 6.93396737, 5.94034525, 7.21577745,
10.84595505]])

array ([[0., 0.45323217, -1.00172885, 3.01899278,
4.99353055], [8.24773555, -5.60380425,
7.41758328, 6.27378038, -16.61359546]])

array ([[0., 2.20637474, -3.99309655,
2.9811267, 3.20414581], [3.03113501, -
6.42420727, 6.60592516, 10.20118591, -
4.875525]])

Each of the arithmetic operations performed is element-
wise. The division operations require extra care, though. In

Python, most arithmetic errors in code throw a run-time error, which helps in debugging. For NumPy, however, the code could run with a warning issued.

Array – Scalar operations

Also, NumPy supports scalar with Array operations. A scalar in this context is just a single numeric value of either integer or float type. The scalar – Array operations are also element-wise, by the broadcast feature of NumPy arrays.

Example:
```
In []: #Scalar- Array Operations
new_array = np. arrange (0,11)    # Array of values from 0-
    10
print('New_array')
new_array              # Show
Sc = 100               # Scalar value


# let us make an array with a range from 100 - 110 (using +)
add_array = new_array + Sc    # Adding 100 to every item
print('\nAdd_array')
add_array              # Show
# Let us make an array of 100s (using -)
centurion = add_array - new_array
print('\nCenturion')
centurion              # Show
```

```python
# Let us do some multiplication (using *)
multiplex = new_array * 100
print('\nMultiplex')
multiplex              # Show
# division [take care], let us deliberately generate
# an error. We will do a divide by Zero.
err_vec = new_array / new_array
print('\nError_vec')
err_vec
# Show
```

New_array

Out []: array ([0, 1, 2, 3, 4, 5, 6, 7, 8, 9, 10])

Add_array

Out []: array ([100, 101, 102, 103, 104, 105, 106, 107, 108, 109, 110])

Centurion

Out []: array ([100, 100, 100, 100, 100, 100, 100, 100, 100, 100, 100])

Multiplex

Out []: array ([0, 100, 200, 300, 400, 500, 600, 700, 800, 900, 1000])

Error_vec

C:\Users\Oguntuase\Anaconda3\lib\site-packages\ipykernel_launcher.py:27:

RuntimeWarning: invalid value encountered in true_divide

array ([nan, 1., 1., 1., 1., 1., 1., 1., 1., 1., 1.])

Chapter 6: K-Nearest Neighbors Algorithm

The KNN algorithm is highly used for building more complex classifiers. It is a simple algorithm, but it has outperformed many powerful classifiers. That is why it is used in numerous applications data compression, economic forecasting, and genetics. KNN is a supervised learning algorithm, which means that we are given a labeled dataset made up of training observations (x, y) and our goal is to determine the relationship between x and y. This means that we should find a function that x to y such that when we are given an input value for x, we can predict the corresponding value for y. The concept behind the KNN algorithm is very simple. We will use a dataset named Iris. We had explored it previously. We will be using this to demonstrate how to implement the KNN algorithm.

First, import all the libraries that are needed:

```
import numpy as np
import pandas as pd
import matplotlib.pyplot as plt
```

Splitting the Dataset

We need to be able to tell how well our algorithm performed. This will be done during the testing phase. This means that we should have the training and testing data. The data set should be divided into two parts. We need to split the data into two parts. 80% of the data will be used as the training set, while 20% will be used as the test set. Let us first import the *train_test_split* method from Scikit-Learn.

Feature Scaling

Before we can make real predictions, it is a good idea for us to scale the features. After that, all the features will be evaluated uniformly. Scikit-Learn comes with a class named *StandardScaler,* which can help us perform the feature scaling. Let us first import this class.

We then instantiate the class then use it to fit a model based on it:

```
feature_scaler = StandardScaler()
feature_scaler.fit(X_train)
X_train = feature_scaler.transform(X_train)
X_test = feature_scaler.transform(X_test)
```

The instance was given the name *feature_scaler.*

Training the Algorithm

With the Scikit-Learn library, it is easy for us to train the KNN algorithm. Let us first import the *KNeighborsClassifier* from the Scikit-Learn library:

from sklearn. neighbors import KNeighborsClassifier
The following code will help us train the algorithm:

```
knn_classifier = KNeighborsClassifier(n_neighbors=5)
knn_classifier.fit(X_train, y_train)
```

Note that we have created an instance of the class we have created and named the instance *knn_classifier*. We have used one parameter in the instantiation, that is, *n_neighbors*. We have used 5 as the value of this parameter, and this basically, denotes the value of K. Note that there is no specific value for K, and it is chosen after testing and evaluation. However, for a start, 5 is used as the most popular value in most KNN applications. We can then use the test data to make predictions. This can be done by running the script given below:

pred_y = knn_classifier. predict(X_test)

Evaluating the Accuracy

Evaluation of the KNN algorithm is not done in the same way as evaluating the accuracy of the linear regression algorithm. We were using metrics like RMSE, MAE, etc. In this case, we will use metrics like confusion matrix, precision, recall, and f1 score. We can use the *classification_report* and *confusion_matrix* methods to calculate these metrics. Let us first import these from the Scikit-Learn library: from sklearn. metrics import confusion_matrix, classification_report

Run the following script:

```
print(confusion_matrix(y_test, pred_y))
print(classification_report(y_test, pred_y))
```

The results given above show that the KNN algorithm did a good job of classifying the 30 records that we have in the test dataset. The results show that the average accuracy of the algorithm on the dataset was about 90%. This is not a bad percentage.

K Means Clustering

Let us manually demonstrate how this algorithm works before implementing it on Scikit-Learn:

Suppose we have two-dimensional data instances given below and by the name D:

```
D = { (5,3)' (10,15)' (15,12)' (24,10)' (30,45)' (85,70)' (71,80)' (60,78)' (55,52)' (80,91) }
```

Our objective is to classify the data based on the similarity between the data points.

We should first initialize the values for the centroids of both clusters, and this should be done randomly. The centroids will be named c1 and c2 for clusters C1 and C2 respectively, and we will initialize them with the values for the first two data points, that is, (5,3) and (10,15). It is after this that you should begin the iterations. Anytime that you calculate the Euclidean distance, the data point should be assigned to the cluster with the shortest Euclidean distance. Let us take the example of the data point (5,3):

```
Euclidean Distance from the Cluster Centroid c1 = (5,3) = 0
Euclidean Distance from the Cluster Centroid c2 = (10,15) = 13
```

The Euclidean distance for the data point from point centroid c1 is shorter compared to the distance of the same data point from centroid c2. This means that this data point

215

will be assigned to the cluster C1   the distance from the data point to the centroid c2 is shorter; hence, it will be assigned to the cluster C2. Now that the data points have been assigned to the right clusters, the next step should involve the calculation of the new centroid values. The values should be calculated by determining the means of the coordinates for the data points belonging to a certain cluster. If for example for C1 we had allocated the following two data points to the cluster:

(5, 3) and (24, 10). The new value for x coordinate will be the mean of the two:

$x = (5 + 24) / 2$

$x = 14.5$

The new value for y will be:

$y = (3 + 10) / 2$

$y = 13/2$

$y = 6.5$

The new centroid value for the c1 will be (14.5, 6.5).

This should be done for c2, and the entire process is repeated. The iterations should be repeated until when the centroid values do not update anymore. This means if, for example, you do three iterations, you may find that the updated values for centroids c1 and c2 in the fourth iterations are equal to what we had in iteration 3. This means that your data cannot be clustered any further. You are now familiar with how the K-Means algorithm works. Let us discuss how you can implement it in the Scikit-Learn library. Let us first import all the libraries that we need to use:

```python
import matplotlib.pyplot as plt
import numpy as np
from sklearn.cluster import KMeans
```

Data Preparation

We should now prepare the data that is to be used. We will be creating a numpy array with a total of 10 rows and 2 columns. So, why have we chosen to work with a numpy array? It is because the Scikit-Learn library can work with the numpy array data inputs without the need for preprocessing.

Visualizing the Data

Now that we have the data, we can create a plot and see how the data points are distributed. We will then be able to tell whether there are any clusters at the moment:

plt. scatter (X [:0], X [:1], label='True Position')

plt. show ()

The code gives the following plot:

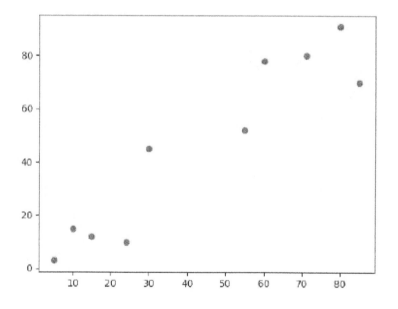

If we use our eyes, we will probably make two clusters from the above data, one at the bottom with five points and another one at the top with five points. We now need to investigate whether this is what the K-Means clustering algorithm will do.

Creating Clusters

We have seen that we can form two clusters from the data points, hence the value of K is now 2. These two clusters can be created by running the following code:

```
kmeans_clusters = KMeans(n_clusters=2)

kmeans_clusters.fit(X)
```

We have created an object named *kmeans_clusters,* and 2 have been used as the value for the parameter *n_clusters.* We have then called the *fit ()* method on this object and passed the data we have in our numpy array as the parameter to the method. We can now have a look at the centroid values that the algorithm has created for the final clusters: print (kmeans_clusters.cluster_centers_) This returns the following: The first row above gives us the coordinates for the first centroid, which is, (16.8, 17). The second row gives us the coordinates of the second centroid, which is, (70.2, 74.2). If you followed the manual process of calculating the values of these, they should be the same. This will be an indication that the K-Means algorithm worked well.

The following script will help us see the data point labels:

```
print (kmeans_clusters. labels_)
```

This returns the following:

The above output shows a one-dimensional array of 10 elements that correspond to the clusters that are assigned to the 10 data points. Note that the 0 and 1 have no mathematical significance, but they have simply been used to represent the cluster IDs. If we had three clusters, then the last one would have been represented using 2's.

We can now plot the data points and see how they have been clustered. We need to plot the data points alongside their assigned labels to be able to distinguish the clusters. Just execute the script given below:

```
plt. scatter (X [:0], X [:1], c=kmeans_clusters. labels_,
cmap='rainbow')
    plt. show ()
```

The script returns the following plot:

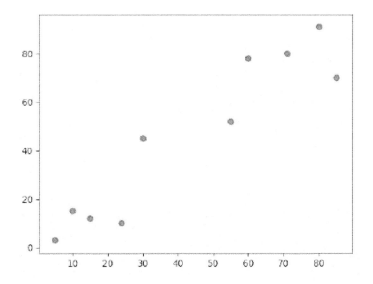

We have simply plotted the first column of the array named X against the second column. At the same time, we have passed *kmeans_labels_* as the value for parameter c, which corresponds to the labels. Note the use of the parameter *cmap='rainbow'*. This parameter helps us to choose the color type for the different data points.

As you expected, the first five points have been clustered together at the bottom left and assigned a similar color. The remaining five points have been clustered together at the top right and assigned one unique color. We can choose to plot the points together with the centroid coordinates for every cluster to see how the positioning of the centroid affects clustering. Let us use three clusters to see how they affect the centroids. The following script will help you to create the plot:

plt. scatter (X [:0], X [:1], c=kmeans_clusters. labels_, cmap='rainbow')

plt. scatter (kmeans_clusters. cluster centers_ [:0], kmeans_clusters. cluster centers_ [:1], color='black')

plt. show ()

The script returns the following plot:

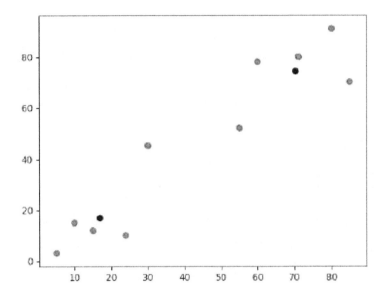

Chapter 7: Big Data

In data science, the purpose of supervised and unsupervised learning algorithms is to provide us with the ability to learn from complicated collections of data. The problem is that the data that is being gathered over the past few years has become massive in size. The integration of technology in every aspect of human life and the use of machine learning algorithms to learn from that data in all industries has led to an exponential increase in data gathering. These vast collections of data are known in data science as Big Data. What's the difference between regular datasets and Big Data? The learning algorithms that have been developed over the decades are often affected by the size and complexity of the data they have to process and learn from. Keep in mind that this type of data no longer measures in gigabytes, but sometimes in petabytes, which is an inconceivable number to some as we're talking about values higher than 1000 terabytes when the common household hard drive holds 1 terabyte of information, or even less.

Keep in mind that the concept of Big Data is not new. It has been theorized over the past decades as data scientists noticed an upward trend in the development of computer processing power, which is correlated with the amount of data that circulates. In the 70s and 80s when many learning algorithms and neural networks were developed, there were no massive amounts of data to process because the technology back then couldn't handle it. Even today, some of the techniques we discussed will not suffice when processing big data. That is why in this chapter we are going to discuss the growing issue of Big Data in order to understand the future challenges you will face as a data scientist.

The Challenge

Nowadays, the problem of Big Data has grown so much that it has become a specialized subfield of data science. While the previous explanation of Big Data was rudimentary to demonstrate the problem we will face, you should know that any data is considered Big Data as long as it is a collection of information that contains a large variety of data that continues to grow at an exponential rate. This means that the data volume grows at such a speed that we can no longer keep up with it to process and analyze it.

The issue of Big Data appeared before the age of the Internet and online data gathering, and even if today's computers are so much more powerful than in the pre-Internet era, data is still overwhelming to analyze. Just look around you and focus on how many aspects of your life involve technology. If you stop to think you will realize that even objects that you never considered as data recorders, save some kind of data. Now, this thought might make you paranoid, however, keep in mind that most technology records information regarding its use and the user's habits to find better ways to improve the technology. The big problem here is that all of this technology generates too much data at a rapid pace. In addition, think about all the smart tech that's being implemented into everyone's homes in the past years. Think of Amazon's Alexa, "smart" thermostats, smart doorbells, smart everything. All of this records data and transmits it. Because of this, many professional data scientists are saying that the current volume of data is being doubled every two years. However, that's not all. The speed at which this amount of data is generated is also increasing roughly every two years. Big Data can barely be comprehended by most tech users. Just think of the difference between your Internet connection today and just five years ago. Even smartphone connections are now powerful and as easy to use as computers.

Keep in mind that we are dealing with a vicious circle when it comes to Big Data. Larger amounts of data generated at higher speeds mean that new computer hardware and software has to be developed to handle the data. The development of computer processing power needs to match the data generation. Essentially, we are dealing with a complex game of cat and mouse. To give you a rough idea about this issue, imagine that back in the mid-80s the entire planet's infrastructure could "only" handle around 290 petabytes of information. In the past 2 years, the world has reached a stage where it generates almost 300 petabytes in 24 hours.

What all that in mind, you should understand that not all data is the same. As you probably already know, information comes in various formats. Everything generates some kind of data. Think of emails, cryptocurrency exchanges, the stock market, computer games, and websites. All of these create data that needs to be gathered and stored, and all of it ends up in different formats. This means that all of the information needs to be separated and categorized before being able to process it with various data science and machine learning algorithms and techniques. This is yet another Big Data challenge that we are going to continue facing for years to come. Remember that most algorithms need to work with a specific data format, therefore data exploration and analysis become a great deal more important and more time-consuming.

Another issue is the fact that all the gathered information needs to be valued in some way. Just think of social media networks like Twitter. Imagine having to analyze all of the data ever recorded, all of the tweets that have been written since the conception of the platform. This would be extremely time-consuming no matter the processing power of the computers managing it. All of the collected data would have to be pre-processed and analyzed to determine which data is valuable and in good condition. Furthermore, Big Data like what we just discussed raises the issue of security. Again, think about social media platforms, which are famous for data gathering. Some of the data include personal information that belongs to the users and we all know what a disaster a Big Data breach can be. Just think of the recent Cambridge Analytica scandal. Another example is the European Union's reaction to the cybersecurity threats involving Big Data which led to the creation of the General Data Protection Regulation to define a set of rules regarding data gathering. Company data leaks can be damaging, but Big Data leaks lead to international disasters and changes in governments. But enough about the fear and paranoia that surrounds today's Big Data. Let's discuss the quality and accuracy of the information, which is what primarily concerns us.

A Big Data collection never contains a consistent level of quality and value when it comes to information. Massive datasets may contain accurate and valuable data that we can use, however, without a doubt it also involves several factors that lead to inaccuracy. One of the first questions you need to ask yourself is regarding those who have recorded the data and prepared the datasets. Have they made some assumptions to fill in the blanks? Have they always recorded nothing but facts and accurate data? Furthermore, you need to concern yourself with the type of storage system that was used to hold on to that data and who had access to it. Did someone do anything to change the data? Was the storage system damaged in some way that led to the corruption of a large number of files? In addition, you need to consider the way that data was measured. Imagine four devices being used in the same area to measure the temperature of the air. All of that data was recorded, but every device shows a different value. Which one of them holds the right values? Which one has inaccurate measurements? Did someone make any mistakes during the data gathering process?

Big Data poses many challenges and raises many questions. Many variables influence the quality and the value of data and we need to consider them before getting to the actual data. We have to deal with the limitations of technology, the possibility of human error, faulty equipment, badly written algorithms, and so on. This is why Big Data became a specialization of its own. It is highly complex and that is why we are taking this section of the book to discuss the fundamentals of Big Data and challenges you would face as a data scientist if you choose to specialize in it.

Applications in the Real World

Big Data is a component of Data Science, which means that as long as something generates and records data, this field will continue being developed. Therefore, if you are still having doubts regarding your newly acquired skill, you should stop. Just think about a market crash. Imagine it as bad as any other financial disasters in the last century. This event would generate a great deal of data, personal, commercial, scientific, and so on. Someone will have to process and analyze everything and that would take years no matter how many data scientists you would have available.

However, catastrophes aside, you will still have to rely on several pre-processing, processing, and analysis to work with the data. The only difference is that datasets will continue to grow and in the foreseeable future, we will no longer deal with small datasets like the ones we are using in this book for practice. Big Data is the future, and you will have to implement more powerful learning models and even combine them for maximum prediction accuracy. With that being said, let's explore the uses of Big Data to understand where you would apply your skills:

1. Maintenance: Sounds boring, but with the automation of everything, massive amounts of data are produced and with it, we can determine when a certain hardware component or tool will reach its breaking point. Maintenance is part of every industry whether we're talking about manufacturing steel nails or airplanes. Big Data recorded in such industries will contain data on all the materials that were used and the various attributes that describe them. We can process this information and achieve a result that will immediately tell us when a component or tool should expire or need maintenance. This is a simple example of how Big Data analysis and data science, in general, can be useful to a business.

2. Sales: Think of all the online platforms and shops that offer products or services. More and more of them turn up every single day. Large businesses are even warring with each other over the acquisition of data so that they can better predict the spending habits of their customers to learn how to attract those who aren't interested or how to convince the current ones to make more purchases. Market information is generated at a staggering pace and it allows us to predict certain human behavioral patterns that can generate

more business and the improvement of various products and services.

3. Optimization: Big Data is difficult and costly to process and analyze, however, it is more than worth it since corporations are investing more and more into data scientists and machine learners.

Chapter 8: Reading Data in your Script

Reading data from a file

Let's make our data file using Microsoft Excel, LibreOffice Calc, or some other spreadsheet application and save it in a tab-delimited file ingredients.txt

Food	carb	*fat*	protein	calories	serving size
pasta	39	*1*	7	210	56
parmesan grated	0	*1.5*	2	20	5
Sour cream	1	*5*	1	60	30
Chicken breast	0	*3*	22	120	112
Potato	28	*0*	3	110	148

Fire up your IPython notebook server. Using the New drop-down menu in the top right corner, create a new Python3 notebook and type the following Python program into a code cell:

#open file ingredients.txt

with OPEN ('ingredients.txt', 'rt') as f:

for *line* **in** *f:* #read lines until the end of file

```
print(line) #print each line
```

Remember that indent is important in Python programs and designates nested operators. Run the program using the menu option Cell/Run, the right arrow button, or the Shift-Enter keyboard shortcut. You can have many code cells in your IPython notebooks, but only the currently selected cell is run. Variables generated by previously run cells are accessible, but, if you just downloaded a notebook, you need to run all the cells that initialize variables used in the current cell. You can run all the code cells in the notebook by using the menu option Cell/Run All or Cell/Run All Above

This program will open a file called "ingredients" and print it line by line. Operatorwithis a context manager - it opens the file and makes it known to the nested operators asf. Here, it is used as an idiom to ensure that the file is closed automatically after we are done reading it. Indentation beforeforis required - it shows thatfor is nested inwithand has an access to the variablefdesignating the file. Functionprintis nested insideforwhich means it will be executed for every line read from the file until the end of the file is reached and thefor cycle quits. It takes just 3 lines of Python code to iterate over a file of any length.

Now, let's extract fields from every line. To do this, we will need to use a string's methodsplit () that splits a line and returns a list of substrings. By default, it splits the line at every white space character, but our data is delimited by the tab character - so we will use tab to split the fields. The tabcharacter is designated\t in Python.

```
with open ('ingredients.txt', 'rt') as f:
    for line in f:
        fields=line. split('\t') #split line in separate fields
        print(fields) #print the fields
```

The output of this code is:

['food', 'carb', 'fat', 'protein', 'calories', 'serving size\n']

['pasta', '39', '1', '7', '210', '56\n']

['parmesan grated', '0', '1.5', '2', '20', '5\n']

['Sour cream', '1', '5', '1', '60', '30\n']

['Chicken breast', '0', '3', '22', '120', '112\n']

['Potato', '28', '0', '3', '110', '148\n']

Now, each string is split conveniently into lists of fields. The last field contains a pesky\ncharacter designating the end of line. We will remove it using thestrip () method that strips white space characters from both ends of a string.

After splitting the string into a list of fields, we can access each field using an indexing operation. For example, fields [0] will give us the first field in which a food's name is found.

In Python, the first element of a list or an array has an index 0.

This data is not directly usable yet. All the fields, including those containing numbers, are represented by strings of characters. This is indicated by single quotes surrounding the numbers. We want food names to be strings, but the amounts of nutrients, calories, and serving sizes must be numbers so we could sort them and do calculations with them. Another problem is that the first line holds column names. We need to treat it differently.

One way to do it is to use file object's methodreadline () to read the first line before entering theforloop. Another method is to use functionENUMERATE () which will return not only a line, but also its number starting with zero:

```
with OPEN ('ingredients.txt', 'rt') as f:

        #get line number and a line itself

        #in i and line respectively

        for i, line in ENUMERATE(f):

                fields=line. strip (). split('\t') #split line into fields

                print (i, fields) #print line number and the fields
```

This program produces following output:

0 ['food', 'carb', 'fat', 'protein', 'calories', 'serving size']

1 ['pasta', '39', '1', '7', '210', '56']

2 ['parmesan grated', '0', '1.5', '2', '20', '5']

3 ['Sour cream', '1', '5', '1', '60', '30']

4 ['Chicken breast', '0', '3', '22', '120', '112']

5 ['Potato', '28', '0', '3', '110', '148']

Now we know the number of a current line and can treat the first line differently from all the others. Let's use this knowledge to convert our data from strings to numbers. To do this, Python has functionFLOAT (). We have to convert more than one field so we will use a powerful Python feature called list comprehension.

```
with OPEN ('ingredients.txt', 'rt') as f:

    for i, line in ENUMERATE(f):

        fields=line. strip (). split('\t')

        if i==0:            # if it is the first line

            print (i, fields) # treat it as a header
            continue         # go to the next line

        food=fields [0]      # keep food name in food

        #convert numeric fields no numbers
        numbers=[FLOAT(n) for n in fields [1:]]
```

    #print line numbers, food name and nutritional values

    print (i, food, numbers)

Operatoriftests if the condition is true. To check for equality, you need to use==. The index is only 0 for the first line, and it is treated differently. We split it into fields, print, and skip the rest of the cycle using thecontinue operator.

Lines describing foods are treated differently. After splitting the line into fields, fields [0] receives the food's name. We keep it in the variablefood. All other fields contain numbers and must be converted.

In Python, we can easily get a subset of a list by using a slicing mechanism. For instance, list1[x: y] means that a list of every element in list1 -starting with indexx and ending with y-1. (You can also include stride, see help). Ifxis omitted, the slice will contain elements from the beginning of the list up to the elementy-1. Ifyis omitted, the slice goes from elementxto the end of the list. Expressionfields [1:] means every field except the firstfields [0].

numbers=[FLOAT(n) for n in fields [1:]]

means we create a new listnumbersby iterating from the second element in thefields and converting them to floating-point numbers.

Finally, we want to reassemble the food's name with its nutritional values already converted to numbers. To do this, we can create a list containing a single element - food's name - and add a list containing nutrition data. In Python, adding lists concatenates them.

[food]+ numbers

Dealing with corrupt data

Sometimes, just one line in a huge file is formatted incorrectly. For instance, it might contain a string that could not be converted to a number. Unless handled properly, such situations will force a program to crash. In order to handle such situations, we must use Python's exception handling. Parts of a program that might fail should be embedded into atry ... except block. In our program, one such error-prone part is the conversion of strings into numbers.

numbers=[FLOAT(n) for n in fields [1:]]

Let's insulate this line:

with OPEN ('ingredients.txt', 'rt') as f:

  for i, line in ENUMERATE(f):

    fields=line. strip (). split('\t')

    if i==0:

      print (i, fields)

      continue

    food=fields [0]

```
try:          # Watch out for errors!

    numbers=[FLOAT(n) for n in fields [1:]]

except:       # if there is an error

        print (i, line) # print offenfing lile and its number

        print (i, fields) # print how it was split

        continue      # go to the next line without crashin
print (i, food, numbers)
```

Chapter 9: The Basics of Machine Learning

As you start to spend some more time on machine learning and all that it has to offer, you will start to find that there are a lot of different learning algorithms that you can work with. As you learn more about these, you will be amazed at what they can do.

But before we give these learning algorithms the true time and attention that they need, we first need to take a look at some of the building blocks that make machine learning work the way that it should. This chapter is really going to give us some insight into how these building blocks work and will ensure that you are prepared to really get the most out of your learning algorithms in machine learning.

The Learning Framework

Now that we have gotten to this point in the process, it is time to take a closer look at some of the framework that is going to be present when you are working with machine learning. This is going to be based a bit on statistics, as well as the model that you plan to use when you work with machine learning (more on that in a moment). Let's dive into some of the different parts of the learning framework that you need to know to really get the most out of your machine learning process.

Let's say that you decide that it is time to go on vacation to a new island. The natives that you meet on this island are really interested in eating papaya, but you have very limited experience with this kind of food. But you decide that it is good to give it a try and head on down to the marketplace, hoping to figure out which papaya is the best and will taste good to you.

Now, you have a few options as to how you would figure out which papaya is the best for you. You could start by asking some people at the marketplace which papayas are the best. But since everyone is going to have their own opinion about it, you are going to end up with lots of answers. You can also use some of your past experiences to do it.

At some point or another, you have worked with fresh fruit. You could use this to help you to make a good choice. You may look at the color of the papaya and the softness to help you make a decision. As you look through the papaya, you will notice that there are a ton of colors, from dark browns to reds, and even different degrees of softness so it is confusing to know what will work the best.

After you look through the papayas a bit, you will want to come up with a model that you can use that helps you to learn the best papaya for next time. We are going to call this model a formal statistical learning framework and there are going to be four main components to this framework that includes:

- Learner's input
- Learner's output
- A measure of success
- Simple data generalization

The first thing that we need to explore when it comes to the learning framework in machine learning is the idea of the learner's input. To help us with this, we need to find a domain set, and then put all of our focus over to it. This domain can easily be an arbitrary set that you find within your chosen objects, and these are going to be known as the points, that you will need to go through and label.

Once you have been able to go through and determine the best domain points and then their sets that you are most likely to use, then you will need to go through and create a label for the set that you are going to use, and the ones that you would like to avoid. This helps you to make some predictions, and then test out how well you were at making the prediction.

Then you need to take a look back at the learner's output. Once you know what the inputs of the scenario are all going to be about, it is going to be time to work on a good output. The output is going to be the creation of a rule of prediction. This is sometimes going to show up by another name such as the hypothesis, classifier, and predictor, no matter what it is called, to take all of your points and give them a label.

In the beginning, with any kind of program that you do, you are going to make guesses because you aren't sure what is going to work the best. You, or the program, will be able to go through and use past experience to help you make some predictions. But often, it is going to be a lot of trial and error to see what is going to work the best.

Next, it is time to move on to the data generalization model. When you have been able to add in the input and the output with the learner, it is time to take a look at the part that is the data generalization model. This is a good model to work with because it ensures that you can base it on the probability distribution of the domain sets that you want to use.

It is possible that you will start out with all of this process and you will find that it is hard to know what the distribution is all about. This model is going to be designed to help you out, even if you don't know which ones to pick out from the beginning. You will, as you go through this, find out more about the distribution, which will help you to make better predictions along the way.

PAC Learning Strategies

While we have already talked about how you can set up some of your hypothesis and good training data to work with the other parts we have discussed in the previous section, it is now time to move on to the idea of PAC learning and what this is going to mean when we are talking about machine learning. There are going to be two main confines and parameters that need to be found with this learning model including the output classifier and the accuracy parameter.

To start us off on this, we are going to take a look at what is known as the accuracy parameter. This is an important type of parameter because it is going to help us determine how often we will see correct predictions with the output classifier. These predictions have to be set up in a way that is going to be accurate but also is based on any information that you feed the program.

It is also possible for you to work with what is called the confidence parameter. This is a parameter that will measure out how likely it is that the predictor will end up being a certain level of accuracy. Accuracy is always important, but there are going to be times when the project will demand more accuracy than others. You want to check out the accuracy and learn what you can do to increase the amount of accuracy that you have.

Now, we need to look at some of the PAC learning strategies. There are a few ways that you will find useful when you are working on your projects. You will find that it is useful when you bring up some training data to check the accuracy of the model that you are using. Or, if you think that a project you are working with is going to have some uncertainties, you would bring these into play to see how well that program will be able to handle any of these. Of course, with this kind of learning model, there are going to be some random training sets that show up, so watch out for those.

The Generalization Models

The next thing that we need to look at in machine learning is the idea of generalization models. This means, when we look at generalization, that we will see two components present, and we want to be able to use both of these components in order to go through all of the data. The components that you should have there include the true error rate and the reliability assumption.

Any time that you want to work with the generalization model, and you are also able to meet with that reliability assumption, you can expect that the learning algorithm will provide you with really reliable results compared to the other methods, and then you will have a good idea of the distribution. Of course, even when you are doing this, the assumption is not always going to be the most practical thing to work with. If you see that the assumption doesn't look very practical, it means that you either picked out unrealistic standards or the learning algorithm that you picked was not the right way.

There are a lot of different learning algorithms that you can work with when you get into machine learning. And just because you choose one specific one, even if it is the one that the others want to work with, using one doesn't always give you a guarantee that you will get the hypothesis that you like at all. Unlike with the Bayes predictor, not all of these algorithms will be able to help you figure out the error rate type that is going to work for your business or your needs either.

In machine learning, you will need to make a few assumptions on occasion, and this is where some of the past experiences that you have are going to need to come into play to help you out. In some cases, you may even need to do some experimenting to figure out what you want to do. But machine learning can often make things a lot easier in the process.

These are some of the building blocks that you need to learn about and get familiar with when it comes to machine learning and all of the different things that you can do with this. You will find that it is possible to use all of these building blocks as we get into some of the learning algorithms that come with machine learning as we go through this guidebook.

Chapter 10: Using Scikit-Learn

Scikit-Learn is a versatile Python library that is useful when building data science projects. This powerful library allows you to incorporate data analysis and data mining to build some of the most amazing models. It is predominantly a machine learning library, but can also meet your data science needs. There are many reasons why different programmers and researchers prefer Scikit-Learn. Given the thorough documentation available online, there is a lot that you can learn about Scikit-Learn, which will make your work much easier, even if you don't have prior experience. Leaving nothing to chance, the API is efficient and the library is one of the most consistent and uncluttered Python libraries you will come across in data science.

Like many prolific Python libraries, Scikit-Learn is an open-source project. There are several tools available in Scikit-Learn that will help you perform data mining and analysis assignments easily. Earlier in the book, we mentioned that some Python libraries will cut across different dimensions. This is one of them. When learning about the core Python libraries, it is always important that you understand you can implement them across different dimensions.

Scikit-Learn is built on Matplotlib, SciPy, and NumPy. Therefore, knowledge of these independent libraries will help you get an easier experience using Scikit-Learn.

Uses of Scikit-Learn

How does Scikit-Learn help your data analysis course? Data analysis and machine learning are intertwined. Through Scikit-Learn, you can implement data into your machine learning projects in the following ways:

- Classification

Classification tools are some of the basic tools in data analysis and machine learning. Through these tools, you can determine the appropriate category necessary for your data, especially for machine learning projects. A good example of where classification models are used is in separating spam emails from legitimate emails.

Using Scikit-Learn, some classification algorithms you will come across include random forest, nearest neighbors, and support vector machines.

- Regression

Regression techniques in Scikit-Learn require that you create models that will autonomously identify the relationships between input data and output. From these tools, it is possible to make accurate predictions, and perhaps we can see the finest illustration of this approach in the financial markets, or the stock exchanges. Common regression algorithms used in Scikit-Learn include Lasso, ridge regression, and support vector machines.

- Clustering

Clustering is a machine learning approach where models independently create groups of data using similar characteristics. By using clusters, you can create several groups of data from a wide dataset. Many organizations access customer data from different regions. Using clustering algorithms, this data can then be clustered according to regions. Some of the important algorithms you should learn include mean-shift, spectral clustering, and K-means.

- Model selection

In model selection, we use different tools to analyze, validate, compare, and contrast, and finally choose the ideal conditions that our data analysis projects will use in operation. For these modules to be effective, we can further enhance their accuracy using parameter tuning approaches like metrics, cross-validation, and grid search protocols.

- Dimensionality reduction

In their raw form, many datasets contain a high number of random variables. This creates a huge problem for analytics purposes. Through dimensionality reduction, it is possible to reduce the challenges expected when having such variables in the dataset. If, for example, you are working on data visualizations and need to ensure that the outcome is efficient, a good alternative would be eliminating outliers.

To do this, some techniques you might employ in Scikit-Learn include non-negative matrix factorization, principal component analysis, and feature selection.

- Preprocessing

In data science, preprocessing tools used in Scikit-Learn help you extract unique features from large sets of data. These tools also help in normalization. For instance, these tools are helpful when you need to obtain unique features from input data like texts, and use the features for analytical purposes.

Representing Data in Scikit-Learn

If you are working either individually or as a team on a machine learning model, working knowledge of Scikit-Learn will help you create effective models. Before you start working on any machine learning project, you must take a refresher course on data representation. This is important so that you can present data in a manner such that your computers or models will comprehend easily. Remember that the kind of data you feed the computer will affect the outcome. Scikit-Learn is best used with tabular data.

Tabular Data

Tables are simple two-dimensional representations of some data. Rows in a table identify the unique features of each element within the data set. Columns, on the other hand, represent the quantities or qualities of the elements you want to analyze from the data set. In our illustration for this section, we will use the famous Iris dataset. Lucky for you, Scikit-Learn comes with the Iris dataset loaded in its library, so you don't need to use external links to upload it. You will import this dataset into your programming environment using the Seaborn library as a DataFrame in Pandas. We discussed DataFrames on Pandas, so you can revert and remind yourself of the basic concepts.

The Iris dataset comes preloaded into Scikit-Learn, so pulling it to your interface should not be a problem. When you are done, the output should give you a table whose columns include the following:

- sepal_length
- sepal_width
- petal_length
- petal_width

- species

We can deduce a lot of information from this output. Every row represents an individual flower under observation. In this dataset, the number of rows infers the total number of flowers present in the Iris dataset. In Scikit-Learn, we will not use the term rows, but instead, refer to them as samples. Based on this assertion, it follows that the number of rows in the Iris dataset is identified as *n_samples*.

On the same note, columns in the Iris dataset above provide quantitative information about each of the rows (samples). Columns, in Scikit-Learn, are identified as features, hence the total number of columns in the Iris dataset will be identified as *n_features*.

What we have done so far is to provide the simplest explanation of a Scikit-learn table using the Iris dataset.

Features Matrix

From the data we obtained from the Iris dataset, we can interpret our records as a matrix or a two-dimensional array as shown in the table above. If we choose to use the matrix, what we have is a features matrix.

By default, features matrices in Scikit-Learn are stored in variables identified as *x*. Using the data from the table above to create a features matrix, we will have a two-dimensional matrix that assumes the following shape [*n_samples, n_features*]. Since we are introducing arrays, this matrix will, in most cases, be part of an array in NumPy. Alternatively, you can also use Pandas DataFrames to represent the features matrix.

Rows in Scikit-Learn (samples) allude to singular objects that are contained within the dataset under observation. If, for example, we are dealing with data about flowers as per the Iris dataset, our sample must be about flowers. If you are dealing with students, the samples will have to be individual students. Samples refer to any object under observation that can be quantified in measurement.

Columns in Scikit-Learn (features) allude to unique descriptive observations we use to quantify samples. These observations must be quantitative in nature. The values used in features must be real values, though in some cases you might come across data with discrete or Boolean values.

Target Arrays

Now that we understand what the features matrix (x) is, and its composition, we can take a step further and look at target arrays. Target arrays are also referred to as labels in Scikit-Learn. By default, they are identified as (y).

One of the distinct features of target arrays is that they must be one-dimensional. The length of a target array is *n_samples*. You will find target arrays either in the Pandas series or in NumPy arrays. A target array must always have discrete labels or classes, and the values must be continuous if using numerical values. For a start, it is wise to learn how to work with one-dimensional target arrays. However, this should not limit your imagination. As you advance into data analysis with Scikit-Learn, you will come across advanced estimators that can support more than one target array. This is represented as a two-dimensional array, in the form [*n_samples, n_targets*].

Remember that there exists a clear distinction between target arrays and features columns. To help you understand the difference, take note that target arrays identify the quantity we need to observe from the dataset. From our knowledge of statistics, target arrays would be our dependent variables. For example, if you build a data model from the Iris dataset that can use the measurements to identify the flower species, the target array in this model would be the species column.

The diagrams below give you a better distinction between the target vector and the features matrix:

Diagram of a Target vector

Diagram of a Features Matrix

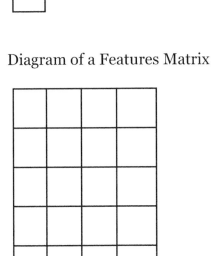

Understanding the API

Before you start using Scikit-Learn, you should take time and learn about the API. According to the Scikit-Learn API paper, the following principles are the foundation of the Scikit-Learn API:

- Inspection

You must show all the parameter values in use as public attributes

- Consistency

You should use a limited number of methods for your objects. This way, all objects used must have a common interface, and to make your work easier, ensure the documentation is simple and consistent across the board.

- Limited object hierarchy

The only algorithms that should use basic Python strings are those that belong to Python classes.

- Sensible defaults

For models that need specific parameters unique to their use, the Scikit-Learn library will automatically define the default values applicable

- Composition

Given the nature of machine learning assignments, most of the tasks you perform will be represented as sequences, especially concerning the major machine learning algorithms.

Why is it important to understand these principles? They are the foundation upon which Scikit-Learn is built, hence they make it easier for you to use this Python library. All the algorithms you use in Scikit-Learn, especially machine learning algorithms, use the estimator API for implementation. Because of this API, you can enjoy consistency in development for different machine learning applications.

Conclusion:

Thank you for making it through to the end of *Python for Data Science*, let's hope it was informative and able to provide you with all of the tools you need to achieve your goals whatever they may be.

The next step is to start putting the information and examples that we talked about in this guidebook to good use. There is a lot of information inside all that data that we have been collecting for some time now. But all of that data is worthless if we are not able to analyze it and find out what predictions and insights are in there. This is part of what the process of data science is all about, and when it is combined with the Python language, we are going to see some amazing results in the process as well.

This guidebook took some time to explore more about data science and what it all entails. This is an in-depth and complex process, one that often includes more steps than what data scientists were aware of when they first get started. But if a business wants to be able actually to learn the insights that are in their data, and they want to gain that competitive edge in so many ways, they need to be willing to take on these steps of data science, and make it work for their needs.

This guidebook went through all of the steps that you need to know in order to get started with data science and some of the basic parts of the Python code. We can then put all of this together in order to create the right analytical algorithm that, once it is trained properly and tested with the right kinds of data, will work to make predictions, provide information, and even show us insights that were never possible before. And all that you need to do to get this information is to use the steps that we outline and discuss in this guidebook.

There are so many great ways that you can use the data you have been collecting for some time now, and being able to complete the process of data visualization will ensure that you get it all done. When you are ready to get started with Python data science, make sure to check out this guidebook to learn how.

Many programmers worry that they will not be able to work with neural networks because they feel that these networks are going to be too difficult for them to handle. These are more advanced than what we will see with some of the other forms of coding, and some of the other machine learning algorithms that you want to work with. But with some of the work that we did with the coding above, neural networks are not going to be so bad, but the tasks that they can take on, and the way they work, can improve the model that you are writing, and what you can do when you bring Python into your data science project.

MACHINE LEARNING WITH PYTHON:

The comprehensive guide to learn and improve Python programming for Machine learning. Artificial intelligence sections with examples and applications included.

William Dimick

Introduction:

Derived from Artificial Intelligence, the concept of machine learning is a complete area of study. It focuses on developing automated programs to acquire knowledge from data in order to make a diagnosis or a prediction. Machine learning relies on the concept that machines can learn, identify trends, and provide decisions with minimal human intervention. These machines improve with experience and build the principals that govern the learning processes.

There is a wide variety of machine learning uses, such as marketing, speech and image recognition, smart robots, web search, etc. Machine learning requires large datasets to train the model and get accurate predictions. Different types of machine learning exist and can typically be classified into two separate categories supervised or unsupervised learning. Other algorithms can be labeled as semi-supervised learning or reinforcement machine learning.

Supervised learning is mainly used to learn from a categorized or labeled dataset than applied to predict the label for the unknown dataset. In contrast, unsupervised learning is used when the training dataset is neither categorized nor labeled and is applied to study how a function can describe a hidden pattern from the dataset. Semi-supervised learning uses together categorized and non-categorized dataset. Reinforcement is a method that relies on the trial and error process to identify the most accurate behavior in an environment to improve its performance.

This chapter will go through the details for each type of machine learning and explains in-depth the differences between each type of learning and their pros and cons. Let's start with the supervised learning that is commonly used and the simplest learning paradigm in machine learning. Before we dive into the details about machine learning when machine learning is the best approach to solve a problem?

It is crucial to understand machine learning is not the go-to approach to solve any problem in hand. Some problems can be solved with robust approaches without relying on machine learning. Problematics with few data with target value that can easily be defined by a deterministic approach. In this case, when it is easy to determine and program a rule that drives the target value, machine learning is not the best approach to follow.

Machine learning is best used when it is impossible to develop and code a rule to define the target value. For instance, image and speech recognition is a perfect example of when machine learning is best used. Images, for example, have a lot of features and pixels that a simple human task is very hard to implement to recognize the image. A human being can visually recognize an image and classify it. But how to develop an algorithm and a rule-based approach is exhausting and not very effective for image recognition. So, in this case building an image dataset and flag each image with its specific contents (i.e., animal, flower, object, etc..) and use a machine-learning algorithm to detect each category of images is very efficient. In short, machine learning is very handy when you have several factors that impact the target value with little correlation.

Machine learning is also the best approach to automate a task for large datasets. For example, it is easy to detect manually a spam email or a fraudulent transaction. However, it is very time consuming and tedious tasks to the same task for a hundred million emails or transactions. Machine learning is very cost-effective and computationally efficient to handle large datasets and large-scale problems.

Machine learning is also best used in cases where human expertise to solve a problem is very limited. An example of these problems is when it is impossible to label or categorize the data. Machine learning in this situation is used to learn from the datasets and provide answers to the problems of the questions we are trying to solve.

Overall, machine learning is best used to solve a problem when: 1) human have the expertise to solve the problem but it almost impossible to develop easily a program to mimic the human task, 2) human have no expertise or an idea regarding the target value (i.e., no label or classified data), 3) human have the expertise and knows the possible target values but it has cost-effective and time consuming to implement such an approach. In general machine learning is best used to solve complex data-driven problems like learning behaviors for clients targeting or acquisition, fraud analysis, anomaly detection in large systems, diseases diagnostic, shape/image, and speech recognition among others. Problems when few data are available, and human expertise can be easily programmed as a rule-based approach it is best to use a deterministic rule-based method to resolve the problem. The large dataset should be available to machine learning to be efficient and effective, otherwise it can raise issues of generality and overfitting. Generality means the ability of a model to be applied in case scenarios similar to case scenarios that served to build the model. When machine learning models are built on a small dataset, they become very inefficient when applied on new datasets that they have not been exposed to. Hence, their applicability becomes very limited. For example, building a model that recognizes an image as a cat or dog image, then apply the same with new images data of other animals. The model will give an inaccurate classification of the new dataset of the other animals like dogs or cat images. Overfitting is when the model shows a high accuracy when applied to the training data, and its accuracy drops drastically when applied to a test data similar to the training data. Another issue with machine learning that should be considered in developing a machine learning model is the similarity between inputs which are associated with several outputs. It becomes very difficult to apply a classification machine learning model in this case as similar inputs yield to different outputs. Therefore, the quality and quantity of data are very important in machine learning. One should keep in mind that not only the quantity of data but also the quality of data affects the accuracy and applicability of any machine learning approach. If the right data is not available, collecting the right data is crucial and is the first step to take to adopt a machine learning approach. Now, you have learned when it is useful to adopt a machine learning approach, when you should avoid machine learning and when a simple rule-based deterministic approach is the simple way to solve a problem. Next, you will learn the different types of machine learning that you might use when each type is applied, the data that it requires, widely used algorithms, and the steps to follow to solve a problem with machine learning.

In supervised learning, we typically have a training data set with corresponding labels. From the relationship that associates the training set and the labels, we try to label new unknown data sets. To do so, the learning algorithm is supplied with the training set and the corresponding correct labels. Then, it learns the relationship between the training set and the labels. That relationship is then applied by the algorithm to label the unknown data set. Formally, we want to build a model that estimates a function of that relates a data set X (i.e., input) to labels Y (i.e., output): $Y = f(X)$. The mathematical relationship f is called the mapping function.

Let's consider we have an ensemble of images and try to label it as a cat image or not cat. We first provide as an input to the learning algorithm images (X) and labels of these images (cat or no cat). Then, we approximate the relationship f that estimates Y according to X as accurately as possible: $Y = f(X) + \varepsilon$, ε is an error which is random with a mean zero. Note that we are approximating the relationship between the dataset and the labels and we want the error ε as close as possible to 0. When ε is exactly 0, that means the model is perfect and 100% accurate, which is very rare to build such a model.

Typically, a subset of available labeled data, which is often 80%, is utilized as a training set to estimate the mapping task to build such a model. The extra 20% of the labeled data is utilized to assess the model's efficiency and precision. At this step, the model is fed with the 20% data, and the predicted output is compared to the actual labels to compute the model performance.

Supervised learning has mainly two functions, namely, classification or regression. Classification is used when the output Y is a quality or category data (i.e., discrete variable) whereas regression is used when the output Y is quantity data (i.e., continuous numerical values). Classification aims at predicting a label or assigning data to a class to which they are most similar. The output Y is a binary variable (i.e., 0 or 1). The example is given above, labeling images as cat or no cat is an example of classification. The model can also be a multi-class classification where the model predicts different classes. For example, Outlook classifies mails in more than a category like Focused, Other, Spam. Several algorithms can be used, such as logistic regression, decision tree, random forest, multilayer perceptron. Regression is used when we want to predict a value such as house pricing, human height, or weight. Linear regression is the simplest model for this type of problem.

The disadvantage of supervised learning is the fact that they cannot process new information, and training should be reconsidered when new information is available. For instance, we have a set of training images of dogs and cats, and the model is trained to label images as dog images or cat images. In other words, we have developed a model with two categories of dogs and cats. When this model is presented with new images of other animals, for example, a tiger, it labels incorrectly the tiger image as a dog or cat image. The model does not recognize the tiger image, but it provides a classification of the image in a category. Therefore, the model should be trained whenever new information is available.

Chapter 1: Python Installation

Python is a powerful programming language developed by Guido Van Rossum in the late 1989s. This language is currently used in many domains such as web development, software development, education, and data analysis. Reasons for its widespread use include:

Python is easy to learn and understand

- The Syntax of python is easy

- Python has its way of managing memory associated with objects.

- Python is not propriety software.

- It is compatible with all platforms (i.e. Windows, Linux, and Mac)

- Can be interfaced with other programming languages

- Many Python libraries and packages are available for data science and machine learning related applications.

Anaconda Python Installation

Step 1: Download the latest Anaconda distribution file from https://www.anaconda.com/distribution/

There are download options for 32-bit and 64-bit operating systems (Figure 1.1).

Step 2: Click on the executable installation file. A welcome screen will appear (Figure

1.2)

Step 3: Click next, read and accept the license agreement by clicking on "I Agree" button (Figure

1.3)

Step 4: Choose installation type (i.e. One user or All users) (Figure 1.4)

Step 5: Choose a location to install Anaconda Python distribution (Figure 1.5)

Step 6: Select all options in "Advanced installation options" screen and ignore all warnings

(Figure 1.6) and click on the "Install" button.

Step 7: Wait until the installation is complete (Figure 1.7) and then click "next" button

Step 8: Now the Anaconda python distribution has been successfully installed, click on the

"Finish" button (Figure 1.8)

Step 9: To check whether the Anaconda has been installed successfully, on command prompt type python, you should see python shell as shown in Figure 1.9

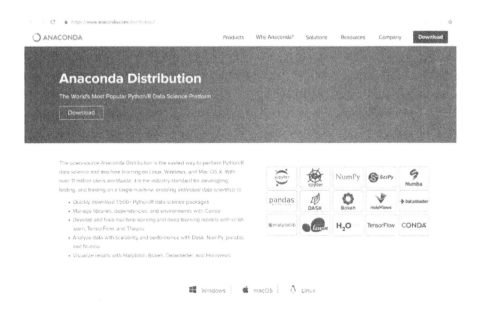

Figure 1.1 Anaconda distribution website

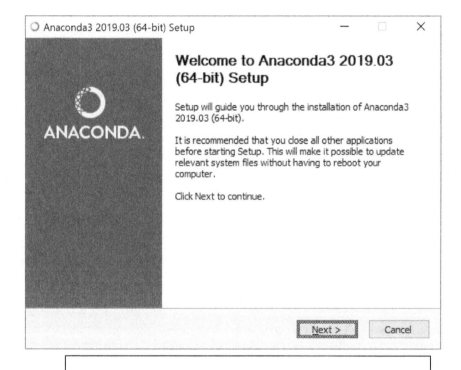

Figure 1.2 Anaconda installation welcome screen

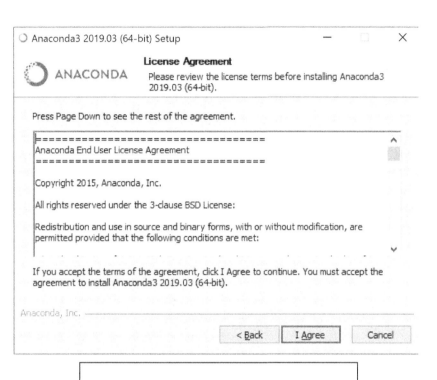

Figure 1.3 License Agreement screen

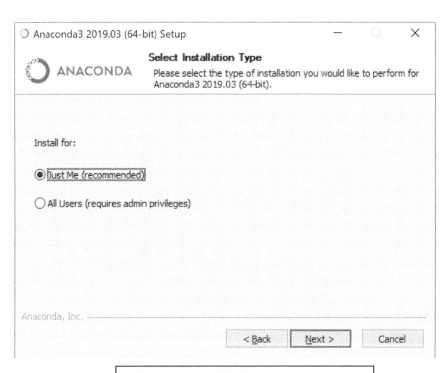

Figure 1.4 Installation type screen

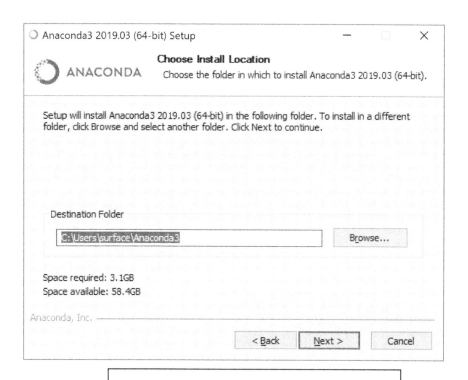

Figure 1.5: Choose destination folder screen

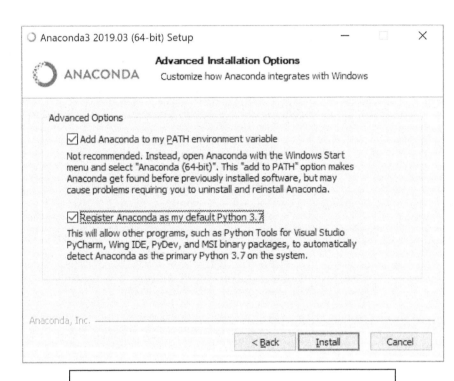

Figure 1.6 Advanced Installation Options Screen

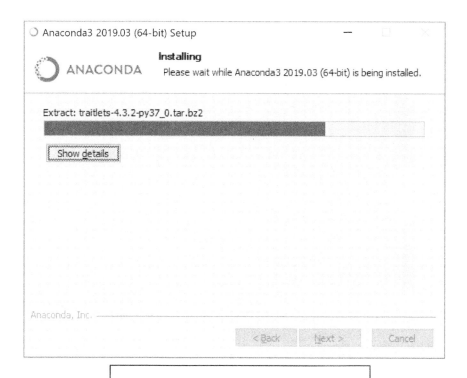

Figure 1.7: Installation Progress Screen

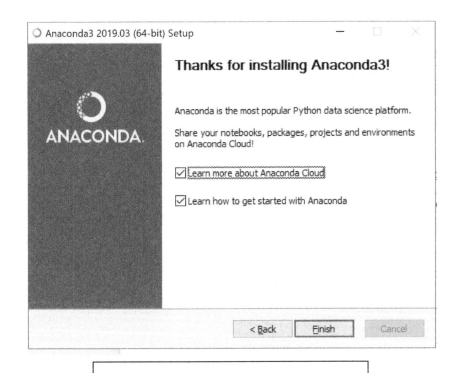

Figure 1.8 Installation Complete Screen

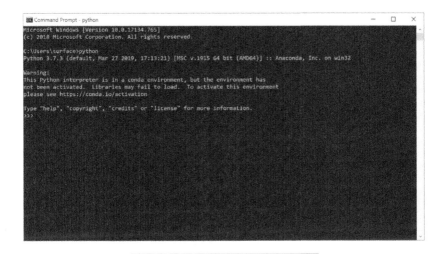

Figure 1.9 Python Shell

Jupyter Notebook

One of the most convenient tools to write Python programs and work with scientific libraries is Jupyter Notebook. Jupyter Notebook is an open-source web-based application. Users can write and execute python code. Moreover, the user can choose, create, and share documents. Moreover, it provides a formatted output which can contain tables, figures, and mathematical expression. To use Jupyter Notebook follow the bellowing steps:

Step 1: Jupyter Notebook is installed with Anaconda Python Distribution. After installing Anaconda, go the start menu, and run Jupyter Notebook (Figure 1.10)

Step 2: After opening the Jupyter Notebook, A "Jupyter Notebook" shell screen will appear (Figure 1.11)

Step 3: After a few seconds, "Jupyter Notebook" dashboard will open in the default browser (Figure 1.12)

Step 4: Now, the user can initialize a new python editor by clicking on the "New" pull-down list and choosing "Python 3" (Figure 1.13)

Step 5: A Jupyter Notebook python editor will be opened (Figure 1.14)

Step 6: Now users can write and execute python codes. In Figure 1.15 a famous "Hello World" code is written and executed

Jupyter Notebook Icon

Jupyter Notebook Shell

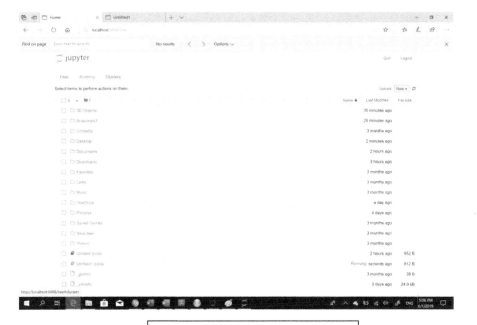

Jupyter Notebook dashboard.

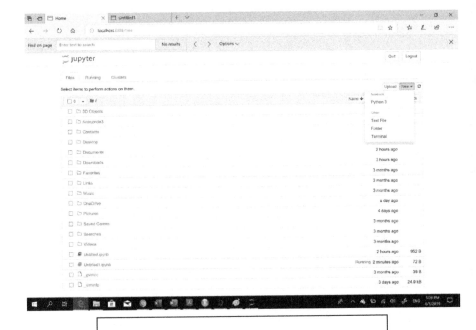

Creating new Jupyter Notebook for Python.

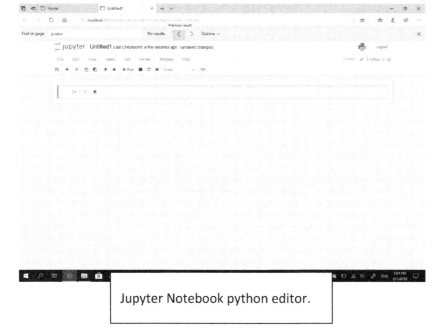

Jupyter Notebook python editor.

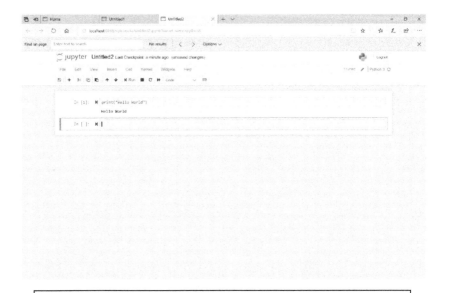

Writing and executing python code in Jupyter Notebook

Fundamentals of Python programming

After learning how to install python, in this section fundamentals of python programming which should be learned for writing basic python programs will be described.

Data Types

In Python, data types are divided into the following categories:

1) Numbers: Includes integers, floating numbers, and complex numbers. Integers can be at any length and are only limited by available machine memory. Decimal points can contain up to 15 decimal places

2) Strings: Includes a sequence of one or more characters. Strings can contain numbers, letters, spaces, and special characters.

3) Boolean: Includes logical values either True or False.

4) None: Represents when the value of a variable is absent

Data Structures

A data structure or data type is a certain method a programming language relies on for organizing data so it can be utilized most efficiently. Python features four of these data types. Let's go over them one by one.

1) Lists: Collections that are ordered, changeable, indexed, and allow duplicate members.

2) Tuples: Collections that are ordered, unchangeable, indexed, and allow duplicate members.

3) Sets: Collections that are unordered, unindexed, and don't allow duplicate members.

4) Dicts (Dictionaries): Collections that are unordered, changeable, indexed, and don't allow duplicate members.

List

Python lists can be identified through their use of square brackets. The idea is to put the items in an orderly fashion separating each item with a comma. Items can contain different data types or even other lists (resulting in nested lists). After creation, you may modify the list by adding or removing items. It is also possible to search through the list. You may access the contents of lists by referring to the index number.

Example

```
In [1]:  ▶ list = ["sam", "bob", "sara"]

In [2]:  ▶ print(list)

           ['sam', 'bob', 'sara']

In [ ]:  ▶
```

Tuple

Tuples use parentheses to enclose the items. Other than that, tuples are structured the same way as lists and you can still bring them up by referring to the bracketed index number. The main difference is that you can't change the values once you create the tuple.

Example

```
In [3]:  ▶ tuple=("sam", "bob", "sara")
           print(tuple)

           ('sam', 'bob', 'sara')
```

Set

When you are using curly braces to surround a collection of elements, you are creating a set. Unlike a list (which is something you naturally go through from top to bottom), a set is unordered which means there is no index you can refer to. However, you can use a "for loop" to look through the set or use a keyword to check if a value can be

293

found in that set. Sets let you add new items but not change them.

Example

```
In [4]:  ▶  set = {"sam", "bob", "sara"}
            print(set)

            {'sara', 'sam', 'bob'}
```

Dicts (Dictionaries)

Dictionaries or dicts rely on the same curly braces as sets and share the same unordered properties. However, dicts are indexed by key names so you have to define each by separating the key name and value with a colon. You may also alter the values in the dict by referring to their corresponding key names.

Example:

```
In [5]:  ▶  dict = {
                "name1":"sam",
                "name2":"bob",
                "name3":"sara"
            }
            print(dict)

            {'name1': 'sam', 'name2': 'bob', 'name3': 'sara'}
```

294

Variable names or identifiers

In python, variable names or identifiers (i.e. names given to variables, functions, modules, …) can include either lowercase or uppercase letters, numbers, parentheses, and underscore. However, python names and identifiers cannot start with digits

Example: In the first example given in Figure 1.16, a variable called "test" is assigned with a value of 2. In the second example, a variable called "1test" is defined and assigned with a value of 2. However, as mentioned above, python does not accept a variable name starting with a digit so here it gives an error. Some predefined keywords are reserved by python and cannot be used as variable names and identifiers. The list of these keywords is given in Table 1.1

```
In [1]:  ▶ test = 2

In [2]:  ▶ 1test = 2
            File "<ipython-input-2-f8b048e1ff71>", line 1
              1test = 2
                  ^
          SyntaxError: invalid syntax
```

Defining variables in python

Arithmetic Operations in Python

Similar to other programming languages, basic arithmetic operations including add, subtract, division, multiplication, and exponentiation can be performed in Python. The arithmetic operators and their corresponding symbols are summarized in table 1.2.

Arithmetic operators in Python

Operator Symbol	Operator name	Operator Description
+	Addition	Adds the two values
-	Subtraction	Subtracts the two values
*	Multiplication	Gives the product of two values
/	Division	Produces the quotients of two values

%	Modulus	Divides two values and returns the remainder
**	Exponent	Returns exponential power
//	Floor division	Returns an integral part of the quotient

Examples: Examples of arithmetic operations in python are given below:

```
In [1]:  ▶  10 + 2
```
```
Out[1]: 12
```
```
In [2]:  ▶  10 - 2
```
```
Out[2]: 8
```
```
In [3]:  ▶  10 * 2
```
```
Out[3]: 20
```
```
In [4]:  ▶  10 / 2
```
```
Out[4]: 5.0
```
```
In [5]:  ▶  10 ** 2
```
```
Out[5]: 100
```
```
In [6]:  ▶  10 % 2
```
```
Out[6]: 0
```
```
In [7]:  ▶  10 // 2
```
```
Out[7]: 5
```

Assignment Operators

Assignment operators are used to assign the values after evaluating the operands on the right sides. These assignments work from right to left. The simplest assignment operator is the equal sign which is used to simply assign the value from the right side to the operand on the right side. All assignment operators are summarized in table 1.3.

Assignment operators in Python

Operator Symbol	Operator name	Operator Description
=	Assignment	Assigns the value of the left operand to the right operand
+=	Addition	Adds the values of right operands to the left and assigns the results to the left
-=	Subtraction	Subtract the values of right operands

		to the left and assigns the results to the left
*=	Multiplication	Multiplies the values of right operands to the left and assigns the results to the left
/=	Division	Divides the values of right operands to the left and assigns the results to the left
**=	Exponentiation	Calculates the exponential power and assigns the result to the left operand
//=	Floor Division	Calculates an integral part of quotient and assigns the result to the left operand

| %= | Remainder | Calculates the remainder of quotient and assigns the result to the left operand |

Examples: Examples of assignment operations in python are given below:

```
In [10]:   m = 2
           m+=1
           print(m)
```

3

```
In [12]:   m = 5
           n = 2
           m-=n
           print(m)
```

3

```
In [13]:   m = 4
           n = 3
           m*=n
           print(m)
```

12

Comparison Operators

Comparison operators are used to compare the values of the operands. These operators return Boolean (logical) values, True or False. The values of operands can be numbers, strings, or Boolean values. The strings are compared based on their alphabetical order. For instance, "A" is less than "C". All comparison operators are given in table 1.4.

Comparison Operators

Operator Symbol	Operator name	Operator Description
==	Equal to	Returns True if the operands on both sides are equal, otherwise returns false
!=	Not equal to	Returns True if the operands on both

		sides are not equal, otherwise returns false
>	Greater than	Returns True if the operand on the left side is greater than the operand in the right side
<	Less than	Returns True if the operand on the left side is less than the operand in the right side
>=	Greater or equal two	Returns True if the operand on the left side is greater or equal to the operand in the right side
<=	Less or equal to	Returns True if the operand on the left side is less or equal to the operand in the right side

Examples: Examples of comparison operations in python are given below:

```
In [14]:  ▶  m = 2
             n = 10
             m != n
```

```
Out[14]:  True
```

```
In [15]:  ▶  m = 2
             n = 10
             m >= n
```

```
Out[15]:  False
```

Chapter 2: Python for Machine Learning

In order to use machine learning, we need a programming language to provide instruction to the machine to execute the code. In this section, we are going to learn the basics of the Python language, how to install and launch python. We are also going to learn some Python syntax and some useful tools to run Python. We also cover some basic Python libraries that useful for machine learning.

Why use Python for machine learning?

Python is a programming language extensively used for many reasons. One main reason it is a free and open-source language, which means it is accessible for everybody. Although it is free, it is a community-based language, meaning that it is developed and supported by a community that gathers its effort through the internet to improve the language features. Other reasons people would use Python are 1) quality as a readable language with a simple syntax, 2) program portability to any operating system (e.g. Windows , Unix) without or with little modifications,3)Speed of execution: Python does not need compilation and run faster than similar programming languages, 4) Component integration which means that

Python can be integrated with other programs, can be called from C and C++ libraries, or call another programming language. Python comes with basic and powerful standard operations as well as advanced pre-coded libraries like Numpy for numeric programming. Another advantage of Python is automatic memory management and does not require variable and size declaration. Moreover, Python allows developing different applications such as developing Graphical User Interface (GUI), doing numeric programming, do game programming, database programming, internet scripting, and much more. In this book section, we will focus on how to do numeric programming for machine learning applications and how to get started with Python.

How to Get started with Python?

Python, a scripting language, and like any other programming language, it needs an interpreter. The latter is a program that executes other language programs. As its name indicates, it works as an interpreter for computer hardware to execute the instructions of a Python programming. Python comes as a software package and can be downloaded from Python's website: www.python.org. When installing Python, the interpreter is usually an executable program. Note that if you use UNIX and LUNIX, Python might be already installed and probably is in the

/usr directory. Now that you have Python installed let's explore how we can run some basic code.

To run Python, you can open your operating system's prompt (on Windows open a DOS console Window) and type python. If it does not work, it means that you don't have python in Shell's path Environment variable. In this case, you should type the full path of the Python executable. On Windows, it should be something similar to C:\Python3.7\python and in UNIX or LUNIX is installed in the bin folder: /usr/local/bin/python (or /usr/bin/python).

When you launch Python, it provides two lines of information with the first line is the Python version used as in the example below:

Python 3.7.1 (default, Dec 10 2018, 22:54:23) [MSC v.1915 64 bit (AMD64)]: Anaconda, Inc. on win32

Type "help", "copyright", "credits" or "license" for more information.

>>>

Once a session is launched, Python prompts >>> which means it is ready. It is ready to run line codes you write in. The following is an example of printing statement:

>>> print ('Hello World!')

Hello World!

>>>

When running Python in an interactive session as we did, it displays the results after >>> as shown in the example. The code is executed interactively. To exit the interactive Python session type Ctrl-Z on Windows or Ctrl-D on Unix/UNIX machine.

Now we learned how to launch Python and run codes in an interactive session. This is a good way to experiment and test codes. However, the code is never saved and need to be typed again to run the statement again. To store the code, we need to type it in a file called module. Files that contain Python statements are called modules. These files have an extension '.py.' The module can be executed simply by typing the module name. A text editor like Notepad++ can be used to create the module files. For instance, let's create a module named text.py that prints 'Hello World,' and calculates $3\char`^2$. The file should contain the following statements:

print ('Hello World! ')

print ('3^2 equal to ' 3**2)

To run this module, in the operating system's prompt, type the following command line:

```
python test.py
```

If this command line does not work, you should type the full path of Python's executable and the full path of the test.py file. You can also change the working directory by typing cd full path of the test.py file, then type python test.py. Changing the working directory to the directory where you saved the modules is a good way to avoid typing the full path of the modules every time you are running the module. The output is:

```
C:\Users>python C:\Users\test.py

    Hello World!

    3^2 equal to 9
```

When we run the module test.py, the results are displayed in the operating system's prompt and go away as the prompt is closed. To store the results in a file, we can use a shell syntax by typing:

```
python test.py > save.txt
```

The output of test.py is redirected and saved in the save.txt file.

In the next sections, we are going to learn Python syntax. For now, we are going to use the command line to explore Python syntax.

Python syntax

Before we learn some Python syntax, we are going to explore the main types of data that can be used in Python and how a program is structured. A program is a set of modules that are a series of statements that contain expressions. These expressions create and process objects which are variables that represent data.

Python Variables

In Python, we can use built-in objects, namely numbers, strings, lists, dictionaries, tuples, and files. Python supports the usual numeric types the integer and float as well as complex numbers. Strings are character chains whereas lists and dictionaries are an ensemble of other objects that can be a number or a string or other lists or dictionaries. Lists and dictionaries are indexed and can be iterated through. The main difference between lists and dictionaries is the way items are stored and how they can be fetched. Items in a list are ordered and can be fetched by position whereas they are stored and fetched in dictionaries by key. Tuples like lists are positionally ordered set of objects. Finally, Python allows also creating and reading files as objects. Python provides all the tools and mathematical functions to process these objects. In this book, we will focus on the number variables and how to process them as we won't need the other variables for basic machine learning

Python does not require a variable declaration, or size or type declaration. Variables are created once they are assigned a value. For example:

```
>>> x=5
```

```
>>> print (x)
```

5

```
>>> x= 'Hello World! '
```

Hello World!

In the example above, x was assigned a number then it was assigned a string. In fact, Python allows changing the type of variables after they are declared. We can verify the type of any Python object using the type () function.

```
>>> x, y, z=10,'Banana,2.4
```

```
>>> print (type(x))
```

<class 'int '>

```
>>> print(type(y))
```

<class 'str '>

```
>>> print (type(z))
```

To declare a string variable, both single and double quotes can be used.

To name a Python variable, only alpha-numeric characters and underscores can be used (e.g., A_9). Note that the variable names are case-sensitive and should not start with a number. For instance, price, Price, and PRICE are three different variables. Multiple variables can be declared in one line, as seen in the example above.

Number Variables

Python allows three numeric types: int (for integer), float and complex. Integers are positive or negative numbers without decimals of unlimited length. Floats are negative or positive numbers with decimals. Complex numbers are expressed with a 'j' for the imaginary part as follows:

>>> x=2+5j

>>> print(type(x))

<class 'complex '>

We can convert from one number type to another type with int (), float () and complex () functions. Note that you cannot convert a complex number to another type.

Python has built-in mathematic operators that allow doing the basic operations such as addition, multiplication, and subtraction. It also has the power function. No, if we want to process a set of values, we would want to store them in one single object as a list. To define a list, we type the set of values separated by a comma between square brackets:

>>> A= [10,20,30,40,50]

We can select one element by typing the element index between the square brackets:

>>> print (A [1])

20

We can also slicer notation to select several elements. For example, displaying the 2nd to 4th element:

>>> print (A [1:4])

[20,30,40]

Note that indexing in Python starts with 0 which is the index of the first element is 0. When using the slicer notation, the element of the second index is not included as in the example above. The value of A [4] is 50 and is not included in the output. To verify the dimension of an array, the Len () function can be used.

The disadvantage of using lists to store a set of variables is Python does not allow to apply the mathematical operations on lists. Let's say we want to add a constant variable to the list X we created. We have to iterate over all the list elements and add the constant variable. However, there is a Numpy library that allows us to create an array of the same type and do the basic mathematical operations. The Numpy arrays are different from the basic list arrays of Python as the Numpy arrays allow only to store variables of the same type. The Nymph library is useful in machine learning to create input, output variables, and perform necessary calculations.

In order to be able to exploit the built-in function of the Numpy library, we must import the library into the workspace by typing:

>>> import numpy as np

Use the command pip -install "numpy" to install this toolbox, if it is not already installed in the system.

To create an array, we type:

>>> A=np.array([10,20,30,40])

Now, we can add, multiply or subtract a constant value from the array X by using the simple mathematical operators:

```
>>> X=np.array([1,2,3,4]) # Creating a vector

>>> print(X)

[1 2 3 4]

>>> X=X+5 # Adding 5 to all elements

>>> print(X)

[6 7 8 9]

>>> X=X*10 # Multiplying all elements by 10

>>> print (X)

[60 70 80 90]

>>> X=X-10 # Subtracting 10 from all elements

>>> print (X)

[50 60 70 80]

>>> X=X**2 # Square of all elements

>>> print (X)

[2500 3600 4900 6400]
```

Chapter 3: Data Scrubbing

Similar to Swiss or Japanese watch design, a good machine learning model should run smoothly and contain no extra parts. This means avoiding syntax or other errors that prevent the code from executing and removing redundant variables that might clog up the model's decision path.

This push towards simplicity extends to beginners developing their first model. When working with a new algorithm, for example, try to create a minimal viable model and add complexity to the code later. If you find yourself at an impasse, look at the troublesome element and ask, "Do I need it?" If the model can't handle missing values or multiple variable types, the quickest cure is to remove the troublesome elements. This should help the afflicted model spring to life and breathe normally. Once the model is working, you can go back and add complexity to your code.

What is Data Scrubbing?

Data scrubbing is an umbrella term for manipulating data in preparation for analysis. Some algorithms, for example, don't recognize certain data types or they return an error message in response to missing values or non-numeric input. Variables, too, may need to be scaled to size or converted to a more compatible data type. Linear regression, for example, analyzes continuous variables, whereas gradient boosting asks that both discrete (categorical) and continuous variables are expressed numerically as an integer or floating-point number.

Duplicate information, redundant variables, and errors in the data can also conspire to derail the model's capacity to dispense valuable insight.

Another potential consideration when working with data, and specifically private data, is removing personal identifiers that could contravene relevant data privacy regulations or damage the trust of customers, users, and other stakeholders. This is less of a problem for publicly-available datasets but something to be mindful of when working with private data.

Removing Variables

Preparing the data for further processing generally starts with removing variables that aren't compatible with the chosen algorithm or variables that are deemed less relevant to your target output. Determining which variables to remove from the dataset is normally determined by exploratory data analysis and domain knowledge.

In regards to exploratory data analysis, checking the data type of your variables (i.e. string, Boolean, integer, etc.) and the correlation between variables is a useful measure to eliminate variables.[11] Domain knowledge, meanwhile, is useful for spotting duplicate variables such as country and county code and eliminating less relevant variables like latitude and longitude, for example.

In Python, variables can be removed from the dataframe using the del command alongside the variable name of the dataframe and the title of the column you wish to remove. The column title should be nested inside quotation marks and parentheses as shown here.

del df['latitude']

del df['longitude']

Note that this code example, in addition to other changes made inside your notebook, won't affect or alter the source data. You can even restore variables removed from the development environment by deleting the relevant line(s) of code. It's common to reverse the removal of features when retesting the model with different variable combinations.

One-hot Encoding

One of the common roadblocks in data science is a mismatch between the data type of your variables and the algorithm. While the contents of the variable might be relevant, the algorithm might not be able to read the data in its default form. Text-based categorical values, for example, can't be parsed and mathematically modeled using general clustering and regression algorithms.

One quick remedy involves re-expressing categorical variables as a numeric categorizer. This can be performed using a common technique called one-hot encoding that converts categorical variables into binary form, represented as "1" or "0"— "True" or "False."

import pandas as pd

df = pd. read_csv('~/Downloads/listings.csv')

df = pd.get_dummies (df, columns = ['neighbourhood_group', 'neighbourhood'])

df. head ()

Run the code in Jupyter Notebook.

```
1  import pandas as pd
2  df = pd.read_csv('~/Downloads/listings.csv')
3  df = pd.get_dummies(df, columns = ['neighbourhood_group', 'neighbourhood'])
4  df.head()
5
```

neighbourhood_West 3	neighbourhood_West 4	neighbourhood_West 5	neighbourhood_Westend	neighbourhood_Wiesbadener Straße	r
0	0	0	0	0	
0	0	0	0	0	
0	0	0	0	0	
0	0	0	0	0	
0	0	0	0	0	

Figure 18: Example of one-hot encoding

One-hot encoding expands the dataframe horizontally with the addition of new columns. While expanding the dataset isn't a major issue, you can streamline the dataframe and enjoy faster processing speed using a parameter to remove expendable columns. Using the logic of deduction, this parameter reduces one column for each original variable. To illustrate this concept, consider the following example:

	gender_male	gender_female	city_london	city_mumbai	city_tokyo
Sam	1	0	1	0	0
Rahul	1	0	0	1	0
Mariko	0	1	0	0	1

Table 3: Original dataframe

	gender_male	city_london	city_mumbai
Sam	1	1	0
Rahul	1	0	1
Mariko	0	0	0

Table 4: Streamlined dataframe with dropped columns

While it appears that information has been removed from the second dataframe, the Python interpreter can deduct the true value of each variable without referring to the expendable (removed) columns. In the case of Mariko, the Python interpreter can deduct that the subject is from Tokyo based on the false argument of the two other variables. In statistics, this concept is known as multicollinearity and describes the ability to predict a variable based on the value of other variables.

To remove expendable columns in Python we can add the parameter drop_first=True, which removes the first column for each variable.

df = pd.get_dummies (df, columns = ['neighbourhood_group', 'neighbourhood'], drop_first = True)

Drop Missing Values

Another common but more complicated data scrubbing task is deciding what to do with missing data.

Missing data can be split into three overarching categories: missing completely at random (MCAR), missing at random (MAR), and nonignorable. Although less common, MCAR occurs when there's no relationship between a missing data point and other values in the dataset.

Missing at random means the missing value is not related to its own value but to the values of other variables in the analysis, i.e. skipping an extended response question because relevant information was inputted in a previous question of the survey, or failure to complete a census due to low levels of language proficiency as stated by the respondent elsewhere in the survey (i.e. a question about respondent's level of English fluency). In other words, the reason why the value is missing is caused by another factor and not due directly to the value itself. MAR is most common in data analysis.

Nonignorable missing data constitutes the absence of data due directly to its own value or significance. Unlike MAR, the value is missing due to the significance of the question or field. Tax evading citizens or respondents with a criminal record may decline to supply information to certain questions due to feelings of sensitivity towards that question.

The irony of these three categories is that because data is missing, it's difficult to classify missing data. Nevertheless, problem-solving skills and awareness of these categories sometimes help to diagnose and correct the root cause for missing values. This might include rewording surveys for second-language speakers and adding translations of the questions to solve data missing at random or through a redesign of data collection methods, such as observing sensitive information rather than asking for this information directly from participants, to find nonignorable missing values.

A rough understanding of why certain data is missing can also help to influence how you manage and treat missing values. If male participants, for example, are more willing to supply information about body weight than women, this would eliminate using the sample mean (of largely male respondents) from existing data to populate missing values for women.

Managing MCAR is relatively straightforward as the data values collected can be considered a random sample and more easily aggregated or estimated. We'll discuss some of these methods for filling missing values in this chapter, but first, let's review the code in Python for inspecting missing data.

df. isnull (). sum ()

```
1   import pandas as pd
2
3   df = pd.read_csv('~/Downloads/listings.csv')
4
5   df.isnull().sum()
6
```

```
id                                 0
name                              59
host_id                            0
host_name                         26
neighbourhood_group                0
neighbourhood                      0
latitude                           0
longitude                          0
room_type                          0
price                              0
minimum_nights                     0
number_of_reviews                  0
last_review                     3908
reviews_per_month               3914
calculated_host_listings_count     0
availability_365                   0
dtype: int64
```

Figure 19: Inspecting missing values using isnull (). sum ()

Using this method, we can obtain a general overview of missing values for each feature. From here, we can see that four variables contain missing values, which is high in the case of last_review (3908) and reviews_per_month (3914). While this won't be necessary for use with all algorithms, there are several options we can consider to patch up these missing values. The first approach is to fill the missing values with the average value for that variable using the fill.na method.

df['reviews_per_month']. fillna((df['reviews_per_month']. mean ()), inplace=True)

This line of code replaces the missing values for the variable reviews_per_month with the mean (average) value of that variable, which is 1.135525 for this variable. We can also use the fill.na method to approximate missing values with the mode (the most common value in the dataset for that variable type). The mode represents the single most common variable value available in the dataset.

df['reviews_per_month']. fillna(df['reviews_per_month']. mode (), inplace=True)

In the case of our dataset, the mode value for this variable is 'NAN' (Not a Number), and there isn't a reliable mode value we can use. This is common when variable values are expressed as a floating-point number rather than an integer (whole number).

Also, the mean method does not apply to non-numeric data such as strings—as these values can't be aggregated to the mean. One-hot encoded variables and Boolean variables expressed as 0 or 1 should also not be filled using the mean method. For variables expressed as 0 or 1, it's not appropriate to aggregate these values to say 0.5 or 0.75 as these values change the meaning of the variable type.

To fill missing values with a customized value, such as '0', we can specify that target value inside the parentheses.

df['reviews_per_month']. fillna (0)

A more drastic measure is to drop rows (cases) or columns (variables) with large amounts of missing data from the analysis. Removing missing values becomes necessary when the mean and mode aren't reliable and finding an artificial value is not applicable. These actions are feasible when missing values are confined to a small percentage of cases or the variable itself isn't central to your analysis.[12]

There are two primary methods for removing missing values. The first is to manually remove columns afflicted by missing values using the del method as demonstrated earlier. The second method is the dropna method which automatically removes columns or rows that contain missing values.

df. dropna (axis = 0, how = 'any', thresh = None, subset = None, inplace = True)

As datasets typically have more rows than columns, it's best to drop rows rather than columns as this helps to retain more of the original data. A detailed explanation of the parameters for this technique is described in Table 5.

Parameter	Argument	Explanation	Default
axis	0	Drops rows with missing values	✓
	1	Drops columns with missing values	
how	any	Drops rows or columns with any missing values	✓
	all	Drops rows or columns with all values missing	
thresh	integer	Set an integer threshold to activate column/row removal, i.e. "4" to remove rows or columns with 4 or more missing values.	
	None	Select "None" if you do not wish to set a threshold.	
subset	variable	Define which columns to search for missing values, i.e. 'genre'	
	None	Select "None" if you do not wish to set a subset.	
inplace	True	If True, do operation inplace (update rather than replace)	
	False		✓

Table 5: Dropna parameters

In summary, there isn't always a simple solution to deal with missing values and your response will often depend on the data type and the frequency of the missing values. In the case of the Berlin Airbnb dataset, there is a high number of missing values for the variables last_review and reviews_per_month, which may warrant removing these variables. Alternatively, we could use the mean to fill reviews_per_month given these values are expressed numerically and can be easily aggregated. The other variable last_review cannot be aggregated because it is expressed as a timestamp rather than as an integer or floating-point number.

The other variables containing missing values, name and host_name, are also problematic and cannot be filled with artificial values. Given these two variables are discrete variables, they cannot be estimated based on central tendency measures (mean and mode), and should perhaps be removed on a row-by-row basis given the low presence of missing values for both these two variables.

Chapter 4: Data Mining Categories

Business analyzes vary greatly in complexity. The simplest and most common form of reporting is predefined and structured reports. They are easy to manufacture or even automatically generated and most reminiscent of presentations. They do not require a great deal of IT knowledge from the user. Their biggest drawback is that they are not flexible.

Flexibility is partially eliminated by ad hoc reports, which represent more complex and interactive queries. These reports require a savvier user.

The next level of analysis is OnLine Analytical Processing (OLAP) analysis. This technique is the most interactive and exploratory of the three techniques listed. It requires a skilled user and a lot of specific knowledge.

Data mining is the most proactive and exploratory analysis technique we know of in terms of analysis. It requires highly trained users.

OLAP and DM define the boundaries of predictive analysis, which is currently one of the hottest software development areas. Companies are trying to build tools that fit between OLAP and DM.

Data mining has evolved into an independent field of science in a short period, which can be used in a variety of fields. Digitization and computerization of all areas of our lives mean that the range of them is only expanding.

In the field of the manufacturing process, we often encounter a flood of data from many measuring devices embedded in the production process. Data mining is used to detect the relationship between parameters in the production process and the desired product property, such as steel quality.

In medicine, data mining is used to predict disease development and diagnosis.

The boom of digital image capture has flooded photos stored on computers and the World Wide Web. Data mining techniques are used for the search, classification, recognition, and grouping of images.

The improvement and discovery of new active substances is the main research activity of the pharmaceutical industry. Data mining is used to predict the properties of active substances concerning their chemical structure, which speeds up and cheap the research process.

Non-trivial computer game makers such as chess, go, and the like rely on data mining techniques to equalize or sometimes even surpass the capabilities of a human player.

In 1997, a computer called Deep Blue defeated chess grandmaster Kasparov in chess.

Following are the seven most typical uses of data in enterprises:

- Finding Profitable Customers - DM allows businesses to identify the customer that is profitable for them, and also discover the reasons why.

- Understanding Customer / Employee Needs - DM is depicted for understanding every entity that expresses any behavior. This can mean examining a web visitor and how they "stroll" through a web site, as well as finding out why they never open a particular part of a page that is otherwise interesting.

- Customer Transition Management - This is a very specific use of DM. It is an attempt to identify the user who is about to replace the service provider and, of course, later to prevent this change. Discovering such users is important in today's saturated developed markets, with virtually no new mobile users. They are the only ones who change the operator.

- Sales and Inventory Forecasting - Sales and inventory forecasting are two of the oldest predictive analytics applications. Here we are trying to predict how much and what will be sold, whether there will be enough space in the warehouse, how much will be my income.

- Creating Effective Marketing Campaigns - Probably, no organization has enough resources to target just about everyone with their marketing campaigns. The ultimate goal of using predictive analytics is to respond to the action because many people are.

- Fraud detection and prevention is one of the most demanding areas of data mining. It allows us to detect illegal transactions or transactions that will lead to criminal activity. This area is still in its infancy and has not yet met all the possibilities. The ultimate goal, however, is to be able to watch live the adequacy of the transaction.

- ETL Data Correction - ETL is an abbreviation of the Extract, Transform, and Load commands used in data warehouses. When we stream data from different systems and fill the data warehouse with them, there are often records that lack an attribute, e.g., SPOL. DM techniques allow us to predict, in real-time, the missing attribute and write it down.

Data mining is divided into two main categories:

- Predictive tasks. The goal here is to predict the value of the selected attribute based on other attributes whose values are known to us. The latter attributes are usually called independent variables. The dependent variable, however, is the attribute we are looking for.

- Descriptive tasks. This category of data mining seeks primarily to describe or find patterns in data sets. Usually, descriptive techniques are used to explore the data and are often combined with other techniques to explain the results at all. A good example of this is clustering, which is often used as the first step in data exploration. If we are tasked with exploring a large database, it can be divided into homogeneous groups by grouping, which can then be easier to analyze.

Within these two main groups, there are four major tasks of data mining, which are outlined below.

Predictive Modeling

Predictive modeling refers to the creation of a model that predicts the value of a predictive variable as a function of independent variables. There are two types of predictive modeling.

Classification is the process of finding a model functions that can differentiate between data classes to sort objects without a class. The resulting model is the result of an analysis of a training data set containing objects of a known class.

The resulting model can be presented in various forms, such as:

- Classification rules (if-then),

- Decision tree,

- Mathematical formulas,

- Naive bayesian classification,

- Support vector machines (from now on referred to as svm),

- Nearest neighbor.

Classification is typically used to predict discrete variables. An example is predicting whether or not a web user will make an online purchase. In this case, the predictive variable can only be in two states (0 or 1), and therefore, it is a classification. Classification is one of the most common techniques and one of the most popular techniques in data mining. At first glance, it seems that it is almost essential for humans, as we are more and more faced with the problem of classification, categorization, and evaluation. The main task of sorting is to study the characteristics of an object (problem) and assign it to which one of the predefined classes belongs. There are several different methods we call classifiers in this technique. Attributes are independent continuous, or discrete variables by which we describe objects (problem). The dependent discrete variable, however, is a class that is determined by the value of the independent variables. The most common use of the classification is to detect fraud, use it in production, select content in targeted marketing and to diagnose healthcare. The classification technique is considered as supervised learning.

Prediction (forecasting, evaluation) can be shown in the case of a share value forecast, in which the predictive variable is continuous. The techniques used for forecasting are:

- Linear regression

- Nonlinear regression

- Neural network

The evaluation technique deals with the continuous evaluation of results. Data entry is unknown; the method classifies this unknown data concerning previous entries in a specific field. Fill it with the same function of other fields in the record. The approach itself is based on the ranking of individual records, which according to the rating, sorts it to a specific place. Examples of assessment tasks include estimating the number of children in a family, the total household income of a family, and the value of life.

The prediction technique is very similar to the rating technique and classification. It differs in that the data are sorted differently, based on predictive future behavior or estimated future value. Historical data is used to build a model that explains the current observation of patterns that are mostly repeated. We can predict from sample observation. Predictive examples include predicting where customers will go to buy in the next six months or forecasting the size of the balance sheet.

The goal of both types of predictive modeling is to produce a model that has the smallest predictive error, that is, the smallest difference between the predicted and the actual values. Predictive modeling can be used, among other things, to predict whether a customer will respond to a marketing campaign, to predict disruption to the Earth's ecosystem, or to judge a patient's disease based on findings.

Analysis of Associations

Association analysis is used to identify and describe strong associations or links in the data. The detected links between the data are typically given in the form of implicit rules. Since there can be many links between the data under consideration, we are only interested in those who have the highest support. Examples of using associations are the discovery of genes with similar effects, the discovery of related websites, or to understand the links between different elements of the terrestrial ecosystem. The most famous example of using associations is a market basket analysis, which aims to link different products that have been purchased together.

Group Analysis

Cluster analysis compares objects into groups without predictive classes or their number, compared to predictive modeling. It is an example of undirected data mining. Groups are formed based on the rule that inward groups of elements should be as homogeneous as possible and externally as heterogeneous as possible.

Group analysis techniques have been applied to a wide range of research problems. Generally, group analysis is a very useful technique when we have a pile of data and would like to break it down into smaller meaningful units.

Anomaly Detection

Detecting records that have significantly different properties from most is called anomaly detection. When looking for anomalies, we must do our best not to identify normal records as anomalies. A good anomaly search system should have a high level of detection and a low degree of misidentification of records as anomalies. This is especially important when such a system is used to prevent credit card fraud. Failure to detect the abuse system causes great harm, but if it detects a legitimate transaction as fraudulent, it causes a lot of headaches for the user.

Chapter 5: Difference Between Machine Learning and AI

One thing that we need to spend some time working on and understanding before we move on is the difference between Artificial Intelligence and Machine learning. Machine learning is going to do a lot of different tasks when we look at the field of data science, and it also fits into the category of artificial intelligence at the same time. But we have to understand that data science is a pretty broad term, and there are going to be many concepts that will fit into it. One of these concepts that fit under the umbrella of data science is machine learning, but we will also see other terms that include big data, data mining, and artificial intelligence. Data science is a newer field that is growing more as people find more uses for computers and use these more often.

Another thing that you can focus on when you bring out data science is the field of statistics, and it is going to be put together often in machine learning. You can work with the focus on classical statistics, even when you are at the higher levels, sot that the data set will always stay consistent throughout the whole thing. Of course, the different methods that you use to make this happen will depend on the type of data that is put into this and how complex the information that you are using gets as well.

This brings up the question here about the differences that show up between machine learning and artificial intelligence and why they are not the same thing. There are a lot of similarities that come with these two options, but the major differences are what sets them apart, and any programmer who wants to work with machine learning has to understand some of the differences that show up. Let's take some time here to explore the different parts of artificial intelligence and machine learning so we can see how these are the same and how they are different.

What is artificial intelligence?

The first thing we are going to take a look at is artificial intelligence or AI. This is a term that was first brought about by a computer scientist named John McCarthy in the 1950s. AI was first described as a method that you would use for manufactured devices to learn how to copy the capabilities of humans regarding mental tasks.

However, the term has changed a bit in modern times, but you will find that the basic idea is the same. When you implement AI, you are enabling machines, such as computers, to operate and think just like the human brain can. This is a benefit that means that these AI devices are going to be more efficient at completing some tasks than the human brain.

At first glance, this may seem like AI is the same as machine learning, but they are not the same. Some people who don't understand how these two terms work can think that they are the same, but the way that you use them in programming is going to make a big difference.

How is machine learning different?

Now that we have an idea of what artificial intelligence is all about, it is time to take a look at machine learning and how this is the same as artificial intelligence, and how this is different. When we look at machine learning, we are going to see that this is a bit newer than a few of the other options that come with data science as it is only about 20 years old. Even though it has been around for a few decades so far, it has been in the past few years that our technology and the machines that we have are finally able to catch up to this, and machine learning is being used more.

Machine learning is unique because it is a part of data science that can focus just on having the program learn from the input, as well as the data that the user gives to it. This is useful because the algorithm will be able to take that information and make some good predictions. Let's look at an example of using a search engine. For this to work, you would just need to put in a term to a search query, and then the search engine would be able to look through the information that is there to see what matches up with that and returns some results.

The first few times that you do these search queries, it is likely that the results will have something of interest, but you may have to go down the page a bit to find the information that you want. But as you keep doing this, the computer will take that information and learn from it to provide you with choices that are better in the future. The first time, you may click on like the sixth result, but over time, you may click on the first or second result because the computer has learned what you find valuable.

With traditional programming, this is not something that your computer can do on its own. Each person is going to do searches differently, and there are millions of pages to sort through. Plus, each person who is doing their searches online will have their preferences for what they want to show up. Conventional programming is going to run into issues when you try to do this kind of task because there are just too many variables. Machine learning has the capabilities to make it happen though.

Of course, this is just one example of how you can use machine learning. Machine learning can help you do some of these complex problems that you want the computer to solve. Sometimes, you can solve these issues with the human brain, but you will often find that machine learning is more efficient and faster than what the human brain can do.

Of course, it is possible to have someone manually go through and do this for you as well, but you can imagine that this would take too much time and be an enormous undertaking. There is too much information, they may have no idea where even to get started when it comes to sorting through it, the information can confuse them, and by the time they get through it all, too much time has passed and the information, as well as the predictions that come out of it, are no longer relevant to the company at all.

Machine learning changes the game because it can keep up. The algorithms that you can use with it can handle all of the work while getting the results back that you need, in almost real-time. This is one of the big reasons that businesses find that it is one of the best options to go with to help them make good and sound decisions, to help them predict the future, and it is a welcome addition to their business model.

Chapter 6: K-Means Clustering

Clustering falls under the category of unsupervised machine learning algorithms. It is often applied when the data is not labeled. The goal of the algorithm is to identify clusters or groups within the data.

The idea behind the clusters is that the objects contained one cluster is more related to one another than the objects in the other clusters. The similarity is a metric reflecting the strength of the relationship between two data objects. Clustering is highly applied in exploratory data mining. In have many uses in diverse fields such as pattern recognition, machine learning, information retrieval, image analysis, data compression, bio-informatics, and computer graphics.

The algorithm forms clusters of data based on the similarity between data values. You are required to specify the value of K, which is the number of clusters that you expect the algorithm to make from the data. The algorithm first selects a centroid value for every cluster. After that, it iteratively performs three steps:

1. Calculate the Euclidian distance between every data instance and the centroids for all clusters.

2. Assign the instances of data to the cluster of centroids with the nearest distance.

3. Calculate the new centroid values depending on the mean values of the coordinates of the data instances from the corresponding cluster.

Let us manually demonstrate how this algorithm works before implementing it on Scikit-Learn:

Suppose we have two-dimensional data instances given below and by the name D:

D = {(5,3), (10,15), (15,12), (24,10), (30,45), (85,70), (71,80), (60,78), (55,52), (80,91)}

Our goal is to divide the data into two clusters, namely C1 and C2 depending on the similarity between the data points.

We should first initialize the values for the centroids of both clusters, and this should be done randomly. The centroids will be named c1 and c2 for clusters C1 and C2 respectively, and we will initialize them with the values for the first two data points, that is, (5,3) and (10,15). It is after this that you should begin the iterations.

Anytime that you calculate the Euclidean distance, the data point should be assigned to the cluster with the shortest

Euclidean distance. Let us take the example of the data point (5,3):

Euclidean Distance from the Cluster Centroid c1 = (5,3) = 0

Euclidean Distance from the Cluster Centroid c2 = (10,15) = 13

The Euclidean distance for the data point from point centroid c1 is shorter compared to the distance of the same data point from centroid C2. This means that this data point will be assigned to the cluster C1.

Let us take another data point, (15,12):

Euclidean Distance from the Cluster Centroid c1 = (5,3) is 13.45

Euclidean Distance from the Cluster Centroid c2 = (10,15) is 5.83

The distance from the data point to the centroid c2 is shorter; hence it will be assigned to the cluster C2.

Now that the data points have been assigned to the right clusters, the next step should involve the calculation of the new centroid values. The values should be calculated by determining the means of the coordinates for the data points belonging to a certain cluster.

If for example for C1 we had allocated the following two data points to the cluster:

(5, 3) and (24, 10).

The new value for x coordinate will be the mean of the two:

x = (5 + 24) / 2

x = 14.5

The new value for y will be:

y = (3 + 10) / 2

y = 13/2

y = 6.5

The new centroid value for the c1 will be (14.5, 6.5).

This should be done for c2 and the entire process be repeated. The iterations should be repeated until when the centroid values do not update anymore. This means if for example, you do three iterations, you may find that the updated values for centroids c1 and c2 in the fourth iterations are equal to what we had in iteration 3. This means that your data cannot be clustered any further.

You are now familiar with how the K-Means algorithm works. Let us discuss how you can implement it in the Scikit-Learn library.

Let us first import all the libraries that we need to use:

import matplotlib. pilot as plt

import numpy as np

from sklearn. cluster import KMeans

Data Preparation

We should now prepare the data that is to be used. We will be creating a numpy array with a total of 10 rows and 2 columns. So, why have we chosen to work with a numpy array? It is because Scikit-Learn library can work with the numpy array data inputs without the need for preprocessing. Let us create it:

X = np. array ([[5,3], [10,15], [15,12], [24,10], [30,45], [85,70], [71,80], [60,78], [55,52], [80,91],])

Visualizing the Data

Now that we have the data, we can create a plot and see how the data points are distributed. We will then be able to tell whether there are any clusters at the moment:

plt. scatter (X [:0], X [:1], label='True Position')

plt. show ()

The code gives the following plot:

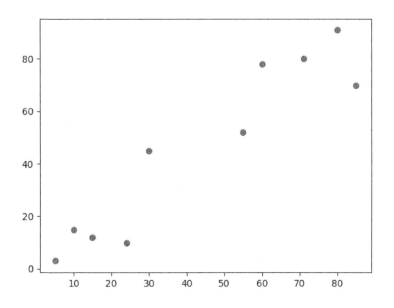

If we use our eyes, we will probably make two clusters from the above data, one at the bottom with five points and another one at the top with five points. We now need to investigate whether this is what the K-Means clustering algorithm will do.

Creating Clusters

We have seen that we can form two clusters from the data points, hence the value of K is now 2. These two clusters can be created by running the following code:

```
kmeans_clusters = KMeans(n_clusters=2)

kmeans_clusters.fit(X)
```

We have created an object named kmeans_clusters and 2 have been used as the value for the parameter n_clusters. We have then called the fit () method on this object and passed the data we have in our numpy array as the parameter to the method.

We can now have a look at the centroid values that the algorithm has created for the final clusters:

```
print (kmeans_clusters. cluster centers_)
```

This returns the following:

```
[[ 16.8   17. ]
 [ 70.2   74.2]]
```

The first row above gives us the coordinates for the first centroid, which is, (16.8, 17). The second row gives us the coordinates of the second centroid, which is, (70.2, 74.2). If you followed the manual process of calculating the values of these, they should be the same. This will be an indication that the K-Means algorithm worked well.

The following script will help us see the data point labels:

print (kmeans_clusters. labels_)

This returns the following:

```
[0 0 0 0 0 1 1 1 1 1]
```

The above output shows a one-dimensional array of 10 elements that correspond to the clusters that are assigned to the 10 data points. You see that we first have a sequence of zeroes which shows that the first 5 points have been clustered together while the last five points have been clustered together. Note that the 0 and 1 have no mathematical significance but they have simply been used to represent the cluster IDs. If we had three clusters, then the last one would have been represented using 2's.

We can now plot the data points and see how they have been clustered. We need to plot the data points alongside their assigned labels to be able to distinguish the clusters. Just execute the script given below:

plt. scatter (X [:0], X [:1], c=kmeans_clusters. labels_, cmap='rainbow')

plt. show ()

The script returns the following plot:

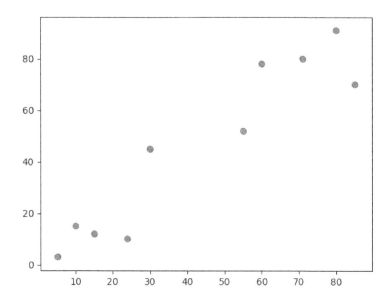

We have simply plotted the first column of the array named X against the second column. At the same time, we have passed kmeans_labels_ as the value for parameter c which corresponds to the labels. Note the use of the parameter cmap='rainbow'. This parameter helps us to choose the color type for the different data points.

As you expected, the first five points have been clustered together at the bottom left and assigned a similar color. The remaining five points have been clustered together at the top right and assigned one unique color.

We can choose to plot the points together with the centroid coordinates for every cluster to see how the positioning of the centroid affects clustering. Let us use three clusters to see how they affect the centroids. The following script will help you to create the plot:

plt. scatter (X [:0], X [:1], c=kmeans_clusters. labels_, cmap='rainbow')

plt. scatter (kmeans_clusters. cluster centers_ [:0], kmeans_clusters. cluster centers_ [:1], color='black')

plt. show ()

The script returns the following plot:

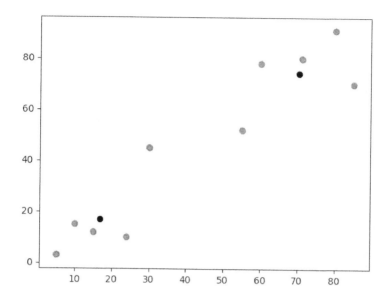

We have chosen to plot the centroid points in black color.

Chapter 7: Linear Regression with Python

The first part of linear regression that we are going to focus on is when we just have one variable. This is going to make things a bit easier to work with and will ensure that we can get some of the basics down before we try some of the things that are a bit harder. We are going to focus on problems that have just one independent and one dependent variable on them.

To help us get started with this one, we are going to use the set of data for car_price.csv so that we can learn what the price of the care is going to be. We will have the price of the car be our dependent variable and then the year of the car is going to be the independent variable. You can find this information in the folders for Data sets that we talked about before. To help us make a good prediction on the price of the cars, we will need to use the Scikit Learn library from Python to help us get the right algorithm for linear regression. When we have all of this setup, we need to use the following steps to help out.

Importing the right libraries

First, we need to make sure that we have the right libraries to get this going. The codes that you need to get the libraries for this section include:

```
import pandas as pd

import numpy as np

import matplotlib. pilot as plt

%matplotlib inline
```

You can implement this script into the Jupyter notebook the final line needs to be there if you are using the Jupyter notebook, but if you are using Spyder, you can remove the last line because it will go through and do this part without your help.

Importing the Dataset

Once the libraries have been imported using the codes that you had before, the next step is going to be importing the data sets that you want to use for this training algorithm. We are going to work with the "car_price.csv" dataset. You can execute the following script to help you get the data set in the right place:

```
car data = pd. read_csv('D:\Datasets\car_price.csv')
```

Analyzing the data

Before you use the data to help with training, it is always best to practice and analyze the data for any scaling or any values that are missing. First, we need to take a look at the data. The head function is going to return the first five rows of the data set you want to bring up. You can use the following script to help make this one work:

```
car_data. head ()
```

In addition, the described function can be used in order to return to you all of the statistical details of the dataset.

```
car_data. describe ()
```

finally, let's take a look to see if the linear regression algorithm is going to be suitable for this kind of task. We are going to take the data points and plot them on the graph. This will help us to see if there is a relationship between the year and the price. To see if this will work out, use the following script:

```
plt. scatter (car data['Year'], car data['Price'])
```

```
plt. Title ("Year vs Price")
```

```
pitlane("Year")
```

```
polysyllable("Price")
```

```
plt. show ()
```

When we use the above script, we are trying to work with a scatterplot that we can then find on the library Matplotlib. This is going to be useful because this scatter plot is going to have the year on the x-axis and then the price is going to be over on our y-axis. From the figure for the output, we can see that when there is an increase in the year, then the price of the car is going to go up as well. This shows us the linear relationship that is present between the year and the price. This is a good way to see how this kind of algorithm can be used to solve this problem.

Going back to data pre-processing

Remember in the last chapter we looked at some of the steps that you need to follow in order to do some data preprocessing. This is done to help us to divide up the data and label it to get the test and the training set that we need. Now we need to use that information and have these two tasks come up for us. To divide the data into features and labels, you will need to use the script below to get it started:

features = car_data. bloc [: 0:1]. values

labels = car_data. bloc [:1]. values

Since we only have two columns here, the 0th column is going to contain the feature set and then the first column is going to contain the label. We will then be able to divide up the data so that there are 20 percent to the test set and 80 percent to the training. Use the following scripts to help you get this done:

from sklearn. model selection import train_test_split

train features, test features, train labels, test labels = train_test_split (features, labels, test size = 0.2, random state = 0)

From this part, we can go back and look at the set of data again. And when we do this, it is easy to see that there is not going to be a huge difference between the values of the years and the values of the prices. Both of these will end up being in the thousands each. What this means is that you don't need to do any scaling because you can just use the data as you have it here. That saves you some time and effort in the long run.

How to train the algorithm and get it to make some predictions

Now it is time to do a bit of training with the algorithm and ensure that it can make the right predictions for you. This is where the Linear Regression class is going to be helpful because it has all of the labels and other training features that you need to input and train your models. This is simple to do and you just need to work with the script below to help you to get started:

from sklearn. linear model imports LinearRegresison

line-reg = Linear Regression ()

lin_reg.fit (train_features, train_labels)

Using the same example of the car prices and the years from before, we are going to look and see what the coefficient is for only the independent variable. We need to use the following script to help us do that:

print (lin_reg. coef_)

The result of this process is going to be 204.815. This shows that for each unit change in the year, the car price is going to increase by 204.815 (at least in this example).

Once you have taken the time to train this model, the final step to use is to predict the new instance that you are going to work with. The predicted method is going to be used with this kind of class to help see this happen. The method is going to take the test features that you choose and add them in as the input, and then it can predict the output that would correspond with it the best. The script that you can use to make this happen will be the following:

predictions = lin_reg. predict(test_features)

When you use this script, you will find that it is going to give us a good prediction of what we are going to see in the future. We can guess how much a car is going to be worth based on the year it is produced in the future, going off the information that we have right now. There could be some things that can change with the future, and it does seem to matter based on the features that come with the car. But this is a good way to get a look at the cars and get an average of what they cost each year, and how much they will cost in the future.

So, let's see how this would work. We now want to look at this linear regression and figure out how much a car is going to cost us in the year 2025. Maybe you would like to save up for a vehicle and you want to estimate how much it is going to cost you by the time you save that money. You would be able to use the information that we have and add in the new year that you want it to be based on, and then figure out an average value for a new car in that year.

Of course, remember that this is not going to be 100 percent accurate. Inflation could change prices, the manufacturer may change some things up, and more. Sometimes the price is going to be lower, and sometimes higher. But it at least gives you a good way to predict the price of the vehicle that you have and how much it is going to cost you in the future.

This chapter spent some time looking at an example of how the linear regression algorithm is going to work if you are just working with one dependent and one independent variable. You can take this out and add in more variables if you want, using the same kinds of ideas that we discussed in this chapter as well.

Chapter 8: Feature Engineering

Feature engineering is, without a doubt, a crucial part of machine learning. In this chapter, we are going to work with different kinds of data, namely categorical data, that we assemble from real applications. This kind of data is extremely common. You've undoubtedly dealt with some kind of application that benefits from it. For example, this data type is often needed to capture information from any kind of sensor or game console. Even the most sophisticated data like the kind that is gathered through complex geological surveys use categorical data. No matter the application, we need to apply the exact same techniques. The main point of this chapter is to learn how to inspect the data and remove all quality problems, or at the very least, reduce the amount of impact they have on the data.

With that being said, let's first start by exploring some general ideas. There are several methods of creating feature sets and understanding the limits of feature engineering is vital.

You'll need to know how to deal with a large number of techniques to improve the quality of the initial dataset. Testing individual features, as well as any combination of them, is also an important step because you should only hold onto what is relevant.

Now let's learn how to create a feature set!

Creating Feature Sets

As you may already know, the most important factor that determines the success of our machine learning algorithms is the quality of the data. Even if we have data prepared by the book, an inaccurate dataset without informative data will not lead to a successful result. When you possess the proper skills and knowledge of the data, however, you can create powerful feature sets. Knowing how to build a feature is necessary because you will need to perform audits to assess a dataset. Without assessing the situation, you might miss opportunities and create a feature set that lacks performance and accuracy.

We are going to start exploring some of the most powerful techniques that can interpret already existing features that will help us implement new parameters that can improve our model. We will also focus on the limitations of feature engineering methods

Rescaling Techniques

One of the biggest issues we encounter in machine learning models is that if we introduce unprepared data directly, the algorithm may become too unstable relative to the variables. For example, you might encounter a dataset with differing parameters. In this case, there's a risk of our algorithm dealing with the variables that have a larger variance, as if there's an indication that there's a more powerful change. At the same time, the algorithms with a smaller variance and values will be treated with less importance.

To solve the problem in the scenario above, we need to implement a process called rescaling. In this process, we have parameter values whose size is corrected based on maintaining the initial order of values within every single parameter (this aspect is known as a monotonic translation). Keep in mind that the gradient descent algorithms are far more powerful if we scale the input data before we perform the training process. If every parameter is a different scale, we will encounter an extremely complex parameter space that can also become distorted when undergoing the training stage. The more complex this space is, the more difficult it is to train a model inside it. Let's attempt to illustrate this metaphorically to stimulate the imagination. Imagine that our gradient descent models are acting like balls rolling down a ramp. These balls might encounter hurdles where they can get stuck, or perhaps a modification in the ramp's geometry. However, if we work with scaled data, we are reducing the chance of having a distorted geometry. If our training surface is evenly shaped, the training process becomes extremely effective.

The most basic example of rescaling is that of linear rescaling, which is between zero and one. This means that our most sizeable parameter will have a rescaled value of one, while the smallest one will have a rescaled value of zero. There will also be intermediate parameters that fall somewhere in-between the two values. Let's take a vector as an example. When performing this transformation on [0, 10, 25, 20, 18], the values change to [0, 0.4, 1, 0.8, 0.72]. This illustrates one of the advantages of this transformation because our raw data is extremely diverse; however if we rescale it, we will end up with an even range. What this means for us is that our training algorithms will perform much better on a more meaningful set of data.

While this rescaling technique is considered to be the classic one, there are other alternatives. Under different circumstances, we can apply nonlinear scaling methods. Some of the most common ones are square scaling, log scaling, and square root scaling. The log-scaling method is often implemented in physics and in datasets that are affected by exponential growth. Log scaling doesn't work in the same way as linear scaling does because it focuses on making adjustments to space between cases. This makes log scaling a powerful option when dealing with outlying cases.

Creating Derived Variables

The preprocessing phase in most machine learning applications, especially neural networks, involves the use of rescaling. In addition to this step, however, we have other data preparation methods that are implemented to boost the performance of the model with tactical parameter reductions. An example of this technique is the derived measure, which uses several existing data points and represents them inside one single measure.

These derived measures are very common because all derived scores or measures are, in fact, combinations that form a score from several elements. For instance, acceleration is a function of velocity values from 2 points in time. Another example is the body mass index, which can be considered as a simple function of height, weight, and age.

Keep in mind that if we have datasets with familiar information, any of these scores or measures will be known. However, even in this case, finding new transformations by implementing our knowledge mixed with existing information can positively affect our performance. Here are some of the concepts you should be aware of when you think about derived measures:

Making combinations of two variables: This concept involves the division, multiplication, or normalization of an n parameter as the function of an m parameter.

Change over time: A common example of this is acceleration in a more complicated context. For instance, instead of directly handling current and past values, we can work with the slope of an underlying time series function.

Baseline subtraction: This concept involves the use of a base expectation to modify a parameter concerning that baseline. This method can be an improved way of observing the same variable because it is more informative. For instance, if we have a baseline churn rate (a measure of objects moving out of a group over a certain amount of time), we can create a parameter that describes the churn in terms of deviation from expectation. Another simple example would be looking at stock trading. With this concept in mind, the closing price can be looked at as the opening price instead.

Normalization: This concept is about parameter value normalization based on another parameter's value. A perfect example of this is the failed transaction rate.

All of these elements provide improved results. Keep in mind that you can also combine them to maximize effectiveness. For example, imagine we have a parameter that says the declining or increasing slope of the customer engagement needs to be trained to express whether a certain customer was barely engaged or well engaged. Why? Simply because of context variety and a small decline in engagement can suggest many things depending on each situation. From this, we can conclude that one of the data scientist's responsibilities is to think of such details when creating a said feature. Each domain has its subtleties that can make a difference when it comes to the results we get. For now, we mostly focused on examples of numerical data, however, most of the time, there are categorical parameters such as codes involved, and we need the right technique to work with them.

Next up, we are going to focus on the interpretation of non-numeric features and learn the right techniques for turning those features into parameters that we can use.

Non-Numeric Features

You will often encounter the problem of interpreting non-numeric features. It is often a challenging matter because precious data can be encoded inside non-numerical values. For example, if we look at stock trades, the identity of buyers and sellers is also valuable. Let's take this further.

This may appear as subtle information, maybe even worthless, however, imagine that a certain stock buyer might trade in a certain manner with a particular seller. Even at a company level, we can spot differences that depend on a particular context. Working with such scenarios is sometimes challenging. However, we can implement a series of aggregations to count the number of occurrences with the chance of developing extended measures.

Keep in mind that if we create summary statistics, and we lower the number of dataset rows, we create the possibility of reducing the quantity of information that our model has access to for learning purposes. This aspect also increases the risk of overfitting. This means that reducing input data and introducing extensive aggregations is not always a good idea, especially when we're working with deep learning algorithms.

There's an alternative to aggregation. We can use encoding to translate string values into numerical data. A common approach to encoding is called 'one-hot encoding.' This process involves the transformation of a group of categorical answers, such as age groups, into sets of binary values. This method presents us with an advantage. We can gain access to valuable tag data within certain datasets where aggregation would introduce the risk of losing information. On top of that, one-hot encoding gives us the ability to break apart certain response codes and split them into independent features that can be used to identify both relevant and less meaningful code for a certain variable. This aspect enables us to save only the values that matter to our goals.

Another alternative technique is mainly used on text codes. This is often called the "hash trick." What's a hash, you ask? In this case, this is a function that is used to translate textual data into a numeric version. Hashes are often used to build a summary of extensive data or to encode various parameters that are considered to be delicate.

Chapter 9: How Do Convolutional Neural Networks Work?

In this chapter, I will explain the theory related to Convolutional Neural Networks, which is the algorithm used in Machine Learning to give the ability to "see" the computer. Since 1998 we have been able to teach autonomous vehicles driving skills, and carry out image classification and tumor detection, along with other applications.

The subject is quite complex/complicated, and I will try to explain it as clearly as possible. Here, I assume that you have basic knowledge of how a feedforward multilayer artificial neural network works (fully connected).

A CNN is an ANN or an artificial neural network that processes the layers in it using supervised learning. It imitates the human eye and brain in the way that it identifies traits and characteristics to identify specific objects. Typically, a CNN has several hidden layers, all in a specific hierarchy. The first layer can detect curves, lines, and other basic shapes. The deeper layers can recognize silhouettes, faces, and other more complex shapes.

We will need:

Remember that the neural network must learn by itself to recognize a variety of objects within images, and for this, we will need a large number of images - more than 10,000 images of cats, another 10,000 of dogs, so that the network can capture its unique characteristics - of each object - and in turn, to be able to generalize it - this is so that it can recognize both a black cat, a white cat, a front cat, a profile

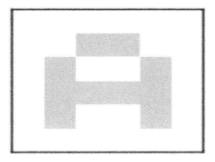

cat, a jumping cat, etc.

Pixels and Neurons

To begin, the network takes as input the pixels of an image. If we have an image with just 28 × 28 pixels high and wide, that is equivalent to 784 neurons. And that is if we only have one color (grayscale). If we had a color image, we would need three channels (red, green, blue), and then we would use 28x28x3 = 2352 input neurons. That is our input layer. To continue with the example, we will assume that we use the image with one color only.

The Pre-Processing

Before feeding the network, remember that, as input, we should normalize the values. The colors of the pixels have values ranging from 0 to 255, we will transform each pixel: "value/255," and we will always have a value between 0 and 1.

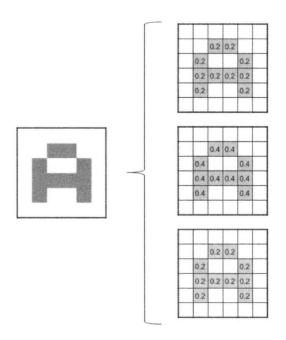

Convolutions

Now begins the "distinctive processing" of the CNN. We will make the so-called "convolutions," which means groups of close pixels are taken from the input image and mathematically operated against the kernel, which is a small matrix. The kernel, for example 3 x 3 pixels, runs the input neurons from left to right a and top to bottom, generating another output matrix, and this will become the next hidden neuron layer.

NOTE: if the image were in color, the kernel would really be 3x3x3: a filter with 3 3 × 3 kernels; then those three filters are added (and a bias unit is added) and will form 1 output (as if it were one channel only).

	0.6	0.6		
0.6			0.6	
0.6	0.6	0.6	0.6	
0.6			0.6	

1	0	-1
2	0	-2
1	0	-1

The kernel will initially take random values (1) and will be adjusted by backpropagation. (1) An improvement is to make it follow a normal distribution following symmetry, but its values are random.

Filter: Kernel Set

ONE DETAIL: Actually, we will not apply only one kernel, but we will have many kernels (its set is called filters). For example, in this first convolution, we could have 32 filters, with which we will really get 32 output matrices (this set is known as "feature mapping"), each of 28x28x1, giving a total of 25,088 neurons for our FIRST HIDDEN LAYER of neurons. Imagine how many more they would be if we took an input image of 224x224x3 (which is still considered a small size).

Here we see the kernel making the matrix product with the input image and moving from 1 pixel from left to right and from top to bottom and generating a new matrix that makes up the features map.

As we move the kernel and we get a "new image" filtered by the kernel. In this first convolution and following the previous example, it is as if we obtained 32 "new filtered images." These new images that they are "drawing" are certain characteristics of the original image. This will help in the future to distinguish one object from another (e.g., cat or dog).

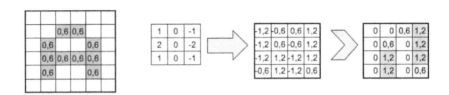

The image performs a convolution with a kernel and applies the activation function, in this case, ReLu.

Activation Function

The most commonly used activation function for this type of neural network is called ReLu by Rectifier Linear Unit and consists of f (x) = max (0, x).

Subsampling

Now comes a step in which we will reduce the number of neurons before making a new convolution. Why? As we saw, from our 28x28px black and white image, we have a first input layer of 784 neurons, and after the first convolution, we get a hidden layer of 25,088 neurons - which really are our 32 feature maps of 28 × 28.

If we made a new convolution from this layer, the number of neurons in the next layer would go through the clouds (and that implies more processing)! To reduce the size of the next layer of neurons, we will make a subsampling process in which we will reduce the size of our filter. There are a few types of subsampling methods available we will see the "mostly used": Max-Pooling.

Subsampling with Max-Pooling

Let's try to explain it with an example: suppose we will do Max-pooling of size 2×2. This means that we will go through each of our 32 images of features previously obtained from 28x28px from left-right, up-down BUT instead of taking 1 pixel, we will take «2×2» (2 high by 2 wide = 4 pixels) and we will preserve the "highest" value among those 4 pixels (so "Max"). In this case, using 2×2, the resulting image is reduced "in half" and will be 14×14 pixels. After this subsampling process, we will have 32 images of 14×14, going from having had 25,088 neurons to 6272, they are much less and - in theory - they continue to store the most important information to detect desired characteristics.

Now, More Convolutions!

Because that has been the first convolution: it consists of an input, a set of filters, we generate a map of characteristics, and we do a subsampling. In the example of images of only one color we will have:

1) Input: Image	2) I apply Kernel	3) I get Feature Mapping	4) I apply Max-Pooling	5) I get «Exit» from the Convolution
28x28x1	32 3 × 3 filters	28x28x32	2 × 2	14x14x32

The first convolution can detect primitive characteristics such as lines or curves. As we make more layers with convolutions, feature maps will be able to recognize more complex forms, and the total set of convolution layers will be able to "see."

Well now we must make a second convolution that will be:

1) Input: Image	2) I apply Kernel	3) I get Feature Mapping	4) I apply Max-Pooling	5) I get «Exit» from the Convolution

| 14x14x32 | 64 3 × 3 filters | 14x14x64 | 2 × 2 | 7x7x64 |

The 3rd convolution will begin in size 7 × 7 pixels, and after the max-pooling, it will remain in 3 × 3 with which we could do only one more convolution. In this example, we started with a 28x28px image and made three convolutions. If the initial image had been larger (224x224px), we would still have been able to continue making convolutions.

1) Input: Image	2) I apply Kernel	3) I get Feature Mapping	4) I apply Max-Pooling	5) I get «Exit» from the Convolution
7x7x64	128 3 × 3 filters	7x7x128	2 × 2	3x3x128

We reach the last convolution, and we have the outcome

Connect With a "Traditional" Neural Network

Finally, we will take the last hidden layer to which we did subsampling, which is said to be "three-dimensional" by taking the form - in our example - 3x3x128 (height, width, maps) and the "flatten," that is, it stops to be three-dimensional, and it becomes a layer of "traditional" neurons, of which we already knew. For example, we could flatten (and connect) to a new hidden layer of 100 feedforward neurons.

Then, to this new "traditional" hidden layer, we apply a function called SoftMax that connects against the final output layer that will have the corresponding number of neurons with the classes we are classifying. If it is dogs and cats, there will be two neurons but, with the numerical MNIST dataset, it will be ten; if we classify cars, airplanes, or boats, it will be 3, etc.

Exits at the time of training will have the format known as " one-hot-encoding " in which for dogs and cats it will be: [1,0] and [0,1], for cars, airplanes or ships it will be [1,0 , 0]; [0,1,0]; [0,0,1].

And the SoftMax function is responsible for passing probability (between 0 and 1) to the output neurons. For example, an exit [0.2 0.8] indicates a 20% probability of being a dog and 80% of being a cat.

How Did CNN Learn to "See"?

Backpropagation

The process is similar to that of traditional networks in which we have an expected input and output (that's why supervised learning), and through backpropagation, we improve the value of the weights of the interconnections between layers of neurons and as we iterate those weights adjust Until optimal.

In the case of CNN, we must adjust the value of the weights of the different kernels. This is a great advantage at the time of learning because as we saw each kernel is of small size, in our example in the first convolution, it is 3×3, that is just nine parameters that we must adjust in 32 filters give a total of 288 parameters Compared to the weights between two layers of "traditional" neurons: one of 748 and another of 6272 where they are ALL interconnected with ALL, and that would be equivalent to having to train and adjust more than 4.5 million values (I repeat: only for one layer).

Chapter 10: Top AI Frameworks and Machine Learning Libraries

TensorFlow

"An open source machine learning framework for everyone"

TensorFlow is Google's open source AI framework for machine learning and high performance numerical computation.

TensorFlow is a Python library that invokes C++ to construct and execute dataflow graphs. It supports many classifications and regression algorithms, and more generally, deep learning and neural networks.

One of the more popular AI libraries, TensorFlow services clients like AirBnB, eBay, Dropbox, and Coca-Cola.

Plus, being backed by Google has its perks. TensorFlow can be learned and used on Colaboratory, a Jupyter notebook environment that runs in the cloud, requires no set-up, and is designed to democratize machine learning education and research.

Some of TensorFlow's biggest benefits are its simplifications and abstractions, which keeps code lean and development efficient.

TensorFlow is AI framework designed to help everyone with machine learning.

Scikit-learn

Scikit-learn is an open source, commercially usable AI library. Another Python library, scikit-learn supports both supervised and unsupervised machine learning. Specifically, it supports classification, regression, and clustering algorithms, as well as dimensionality reduction, model selection, and preprocessing.

It's built on the NumPY, matplotlib, and SciPy libraries, and in fact, the name "scikit-learn" is a play on "SciPy Toolkit."

Scikit-learn markets itself as "simple and efficient tools for data mining and data analysis" that is "accessible to everybody, and reusable in various contexts."

To support these claims, scikit-learn offers an extensive user guide so that data scientists can quickly access resources on anything from multiclass and multilabel algorithms to covariance estimation.

AI as a Data Analyst

AI, and specifically machine learning, has advanced to a point where it can perform the day-to-day analysis that most business people require. Does this mean that data scientists and analysts should fear for their jobs?

We don't think so. With self-service analytics, machine learning algorithms can handle the reporting grunt work so that analysts and data scientists can focus their time on the advanced tasks that leverage their degrees and skillsets. Plus, business people won't need to wait around for the answers they need.

Theano

"A Python library that allows you to define, optimize, and evaluate mathematical expressions involving multi-dimensional arrays efficiently"

Theano is a Python library and optimizing compiler designed for manipulating and evaluating expressions. In particular, Theano evaluates matrix-valued expressions.

Speed is one of Theano's strongest suits. It can compete toe-to-toe with the speed of hand-crafted C language implementations that involve a lot of data. By taking advantage of recent GPUs, Theano has also been able to top C on a CPU by a significant degree.

By pairing elements of a computer algebra system (CAS) with elements of an optimizing compiler, Theano provides an ideal environment for tasks where complicated mathematical expressions require repeated, fast evaluation.

It can minimize extraneous compilation and analysis while providing important symbolic features.

Even though new development has ceased for Theano, it's still a powerful and efficient platform for deep learning.

Theano is a machine learning library that can help you define and optimize mathematical expressions with ease.

Caffe

Caffe is an open deep learning framework developed by Berkeley AI Research in collaboration with community contributors, and it offers both models and worked examples for deep learning.

Caffe prioritizes expression, speed, and modularity in its framework. In fact, its architecture supports configuration-defined models and optimization without hard coding, as well as the ability to switch between CPU and GPU.

Plus, Caffe is highly adaptive to research experiments and industry deployments because it can process over 60M images per day with a single NVIDIA K40 GPU— one of the fastest convnet implementations available, according to Caffe.

Caffe's language is C++ and CUDA with Command line, Python, and MATLAB interfaces. Caffe's Berkeley Vision and Learning Center models are licensed for unrestricted use, and their Model Zoo offers an open collection of deep models designed to share innovation and research.

Caffe is an open deep learning framework and AI library developed by Berkeley.

Keras

Keras is a high-level neural network API that can run on top of TensorFlow, Microsoft Cognitive Toolkit, or Theano. This Python deep learning library facilitates fast experimentation and claims that "being able to go from idea to result with the least possible delay is key to doing good research."

Instead of an end-to-end machine learning framework, Keras operates as a user-friendly, easily extensible interface that supports modularity and total expressiveness. Standalone modules — such as neural layers, cost functions, and more — can be combined with few restrictions, and new modules are easy to add.

With consistent and simple APIs, user actions are minimized for common use cases. It can run in both CPU and GPU as well.

Keras is a python deep learning library that runs on top of other prominent machine learning libraries.

Microsoft Cognitive Toolkit

"A free, easy-to-use, open-source, commercial-grade toolkit that trains deep learning algorithms to learn like the human brain."

Previously known as Microsoft CNTK, Microsoft Cognitive Toolkit is an open source deep learning library designed to support robust, commercial-grade datasets and algorithms.

With big-name clients like Skype, Cortana, and Bing, Microsoft Cognitive Toolkit offers efficient scalability from a single CPU to GPUs to multiple machines— without sacrificing a quality degree of speed and accuracy.

Microsoft Cognitive Toolkit supports C++, Python, C#, and BrainScript. It offers pre-built algorithms for training, all of which can be customized, though you can use always use your own. Customization opportunities extend to parameters, algorithms, and networks.

Microsoft Cognitive Toolkit is a free and open-source AI library that's designed to train deep learning algorithms like the human brain.

PyTorch

"An open source deep learning platform that provides a seamless path from research prototyping to production deployment."

PyTorch is an open source machine learning library for Python that was developed mainly by Facebook's AI research group.

PyTorch supports both CPU and GPU computations and offers scalable distributed training and performance optimization in research and production. It's two high-level features include tensor computation (similar to NumPy) with GPU acceleration and deep neural networks built on a tape-based autodiff system.

With extensive tools and libraries, PyTorch provides plenty of resources to support development, including:

AllenNLP, an open source research library designed to evaluate deep learning models for natural language processing.

ELF, a game research platform that allows developers to train and test algorithms in different game environments.

Glow, a machine learning compiler that enhances performance for deep learning frameworks on various hardware platforms.

PyTorch is a deep learning platform and AI library for research prototyping and production deployment.

Torch

Similar to PyTorch, Torch is a Tensor library that's similar to NumPy and also supports GPU (in fact, Torch proclaims that they put GPUs "first"). Unlike PyTorch, Torch is wrapped in LuaJIT, with an underlying C/CUDA implementation.

A scientific computing framework, Torch prioritizes speed, flexibility, and simplicity when it comes to building algorithms.

With popular neural networks and optimization libraries, Torch provides users with libraries that are easy to use while enabling flexible implementation of complex neural network topologies. Torch is an AI framework for computing with LuaJIT.

Chapter 11: The Future of Machine Learning

In today's economy, all business is becoming data business. In a study conducted by Forrester Consulting, 98 percent of organizations said that analytics are important to driving business priorities, yet fewer than 40 percent of workloads are leveraging advanced analytics or artificial intelligence. Machine learning offers a way companies can extract greater value from their data to increase revenue, gain competitive advantage and cut costs.

Machine learning is a form of predictive analytics that advances organizations up the business intelligence (BI) maturity curve, moving from exclusive reliance on descriptive analytics focused on the past to include forward-looking, autonomous decision support. The technology has been around for decades, but the excitement around new approaches and products is spurring many companies to look at it anew.

Analytic solutions based on machine learning often operate in real time, adding a new dimension to BI. While old models will continue to supply key reports and analysis to senior decision-makers, real-time analytics brings information to employees "on the front lines" to improve performance hour-by-hour.

In machine learning—a branch of artificial intelligence—systems are "trained" to use specialized algorithms to study, learn and make predictions and recommendations from huge data troves. Predictive models exposed to new data can adapt without human intervention, learning from previous iterations to produce ever more reliable and repeatable decisions and results.

Over time, this iteration makes systems "smarter", increasingly able to uncover hidden insights, historical relationships and trends, and reveal new opportunities in everything from shopper preferences to supply chain optimization to oil discovery. Most importantly, machine learning enables companies to do more with Big Data and incorporate new capabilities such as IoT analytics.

Machine learning is a powerful analytics technology that's available right now. Many new commercial and open-source solutions for machine learning are available, along with a rich ecosystem for developers. Chances are good your organization is already using the approach somewhere, such as for spam filtering. Applying machine learning and analytics more widely lets you respond more quickly to dynamic situations and get greater value from your fast-growing troves of data.

Predictive Analytics is Everywhere

A big reason for the growing popularity of advanced analytics based on machine learning is that it can deliver business benefits in virtually every industry. Wherever large amounts of data and predictive models need regular adjustment, machine learning makes sense.

Providing recommendations for books, films, clothing and dozens of other categories is a familiar example of machine learning in action. But there are many more.

In retail, machine learning and RFID tagging enable greatly improved inventory management. Simply keeping track of an item's location items is a big challenge, as is matching physical inventory with book inventory. With machine learning, the data used to solve these problems can also improve product placement and influence customer behavior. For example, the system could scan the physical store for out-of-place inventory in order to relocate it, or identify items that are selling well and move them to a more visible spot in the store.

When machine learning is combined with linguistic rules, companies can scan social media to determine what customers are saying about their brand and their products. It can even find hidden, underlying patterns that might indicate excitement or frustration with a particular product.

The technology is already playing a crucial role in applications that involve sensors. Machine learning also is essential for self-driving vehicles, where data from multiple sensors must be coordinated in real time in order to ensure safe decisions.

Machine learning can help analyze geographical data to uncover patterns that can more accurately predict the likelihood that a particular site would be the right location for generating wind or solar

These are a few of many examples of machine learning in action. It is a proven technique that is delivering valuable results right now.

Distinct Competitive Advantage

Machine learning can provide companies with a competitive edge by solving problems and uncovering insights faster and more easily than conventional analytics. It is especially good at delivering value in three types of situations.

The solution to a problem changes over time: Tracking a brand's reputation via social media is a good example. Demographics of individual platforms shift; new platforms appear. Changes like these create havoc and force constant revisions for marketers using rules-based analytics to hit the right targets with the right messages. In contrast, machine learning models adapt easily, delivering reliable results over time and freeing resources to solve other problems.

The solution varies from situation to situation: In medicine, for instance. a patient's personal or family history, age, sex, lifestyle, allergies to certain medications and many other factors make every case different. Machine learning can take all these into account to deliver personalized diagnosis and treatment, while optimizing healthcare resources.

The solution exceeds human ability: People can recognize many things, like voices, friend's faces, certain objects, etc. voices, but may not be able to explain why. The problem? Too many variables. By sifting and categorizing many examples, machine learning can objectively learn to recognize and identify specific external variables that, for example, give a voice its character. (pitch, volume, harmonic overtones, etc.)

The competitive advantage comes from developing machines that don't rely on human sensing, description, intervention, or interaction to solve a new class of decisions. This capability opens up new opportunity many fields, including medicine (cancer screening), manufacturing (defect assessment), and transportation (using sound as an additional cue for driving safety).

Faster and Less Expensive

Compared with other analytic approaches, machine learning offers several advantages to IT, data scientists, various line of business groups and their organizations.

Machine learning is nimble and flexible with new data. Rules-based systems do well in static situations, but machine learning excels when data is constantly changing or being added. That's because it eliminates the need to constantly tweak a system or add rules to get the desired results. This saves development time, and greatly reduces the need for major changes.

Personnel costs for machine learning typically are lower over the long run than conventional analytics. At the beginning, of course, companies must hire highly skilled specialists in probability, statistics, machine learning algorithms, AI training methods, among others. But once machine learning is up and running, predictive models can adjust themselves, meaning fewer humans are needed to tweak for accuracy and reliability.

Another advantage is scalability. Machine learning algorithms are built with parallelism in mind and therefore scale better, which ultimately means faster answers to business problems. Systems that rely on human interaction also don't scale as well. Machine learning minimizes the need to constantly go back to people for decisions.

Finally, machine learning applications can cost less to run than other types of advanced analytics. Many machine learning techniques easily scale to multiple machines instead of a single, expensive high-end platform.

Getting Started with Machine Learning

Success in stepping up to machine learning begins with identifying a business problem where the technology can have a clear, measurable impact. Once a suitable project is identified, organizations must deploy specialists and choose an appropriate technique to teach systems how to think and act. These include:

Supervised learning: The system is given example inputs and outputs, then tasked to form general rules of behavior. Example: The recommendation systems of most major brands use supervised learning to boost the relevance of suggestions and increase sales.

Semi-supervised learning: The system is typically given a small amount of labeled data (with the "right answer") and a much larger amount of unlabeled data. This mode has the same use cases as supervised learning but is less costly due to lower data costs. It is usually the best choice when the input data is expected to change over time, such as with commodity trading, social media or weather-related situations, for example.

Unsupervised learning: Here, the system simply examines the data looking for structure and patterns. This mode can be used to discover patterns that would otherwise go undiscovered, such as in-store buying behavior that could drive changes in product placement to increase sales.

Reinforcement learning: In this approach, the system is placed in an interactive, changing environment, given a task and provided with feedback in the form of "punishments" and "rewards." This technique has been used with great success to train factory robots to identify objects.

Regardless of your project, an organization's advancement to effectively leveraging machine learning in analytics depends on mastering these foundational practices.

Powerful Processors Are Only the Beginning

Intel helps companies put machine learning to work in real-world applications that demand high-speed performance. It does so with a systems approach that includes processors, optimized software and support for developers and a huge ecosystem of industry partners.

Machine learning requires high computing horsepower. Intel® Xeon® processors provide a scalable baseline, and the Intel® Xeon Phi™ processor is specifically designed for the highly parallel workloads typical of machine learning, as well as machine learning's memory and fabric (networking) needs. In one Intel test, this processor delivered a 50x reduction in system training time.1   Intel hardware technology also incorporates programmable and fixed accelerators, memory, storage, and networking capabilities.

In addition, Intel offers the software support that enables IT organizations to move from business problem to solution effectively and efficiently. This support includes:

Libraries and languages with building blocks optimized on Intel Xeon processors. These include the Intel® Math Kernel Library (Intel® MKL) and the Intel® Data Analytics Acceleration Library (Intel® DAAL), as well as the Intel Distribution for Python*.

Optimized frameworks to simplify development, including Apache Spark*, Caffe*, Torch* and TensorFlow*. Intel enables both open-source and commercial software that lets companies take advantage of the latest processors and system features as soon as they are commercially available.

Software development kits (SDKs), including Intel® Nervana™ technology, TAP and the Intel® Deep Learning SDK. This provides a set of application interfaces so the developer can immediately take advantage of the best machine learning algorithms.

When it comes to to optimization, Intel takes multiple approaches. Including coaching customers and vendor partners on ways to make their machine learning code run faster on Intel hardware, as well as implementing some learning functions in silicon, which is always faster.

Conclusion:

Now that we have come to the end of the book, I hope you have gathered a basic understanding of what machine learning is and how you can build a machine learning model in Python. One of the best ways to begin building a machine learning model is to practice the code in the book, and also try to write similar code to solve other problems. It is important to remember that the more you practice, the better you will get. The best way to go about this is to begin working on simple problem statements and solve them using the different algorithms. You can also try to solve these problems by identifying newer ways to solve the problem. Once you get a hang of the basic problems, you can try using some advanced methods to solve those problems.

Thanks for reading to the end!

Python Machine Learning may be the answer that you are looking for when it comes to all of these needs and more. It is a simple process that can teach your machine how to learn on its own, similar to what the human mind can do, but much faster and more efficient. It has been a game-changer in many industries, and this guidebook tried to show you the exact steps that you can take to make this happen.

There is just so much that a programmer can do when it comes to using Machine Learning in their coding, and when you add it together with the Python coding language, you can take it even further, even as a beginner.

The next step is to start putting some of the knowledge that we discussed in this guidebook to good use. There are a lot of great things that you can do when it comes to Machine Learning, and when we can combine it with the Python language, there is nothing that we can't do when it comes to training our machine or our computer.

This guidebook took some time to explore a lot of the different things that you can do when it comes to Python Machine Learning. We looked at what Machine Learning is all about, how to work with it, and even a crash course on using the Python language for the first time. Once that was done, we moved right into combining the two of these to work with a variety of Python libraries to get the work done.

You should always work towards exploring different functions and features in Python, and also try to learn more about the different libraries like SciPy, NumPy, PyRobotics, and Graphical User Interface packages that you will be using to build different models.

Python is a high-level language which is both interpreters based and object-oriented. This makes it easy for anybody to understand how the language works. You can also extend the programs that you build in Python onto other platforms. Most of the inbuilt libraries in Python offer a variety of functions that make it easier to work with large data sets.

You will now have gathered that machine learning is a complex concept that can easily be understood. It is not a black box that has undecipherable terms, incomprehensible graphs, or difficult concepts. Machine learning is easy to understand, and I hope the book has helped you understand the basics of machine learning. You can now begin working on programming and building models in Python. Ensure that you diligently practice since that is the only way you can improve your skills as a programmer.

If you have ever wanted to learn how to work with the Python coding language, or you want to see what Machine Learning can do for you, then this guidebook is the ultimate tool that you need! Take a chance to read through it and see just how powerful Python Machine Learning can be for you.

Printed in Great Britain
by Amazon